Math Games & Activities from around the World

Claudia Zaslavsky

Zaslavsky, Claudia.
Math games and activities from around the world / Claudia Zaslavsky
p. cm.
Includes bibliographical references (p. 144 – 145).
Summary: Presents games and other activities from different countries and cultures that teach a variety of basic mathematical concepts.
ISBN 1-55652-287-8
1. Mathematical recreations—Juvenile literature.
[1. Mathematical recreations 2. Games.] I. Title.
QA95.z37 1998
793.7'4—dc21

Cover, interior design, and illustrations by Mel Kupfer

Photo credits: p. 20—D. W. Crowe; p. 102 courtesy of the Kenya Mission to the U. N.; pp. 21, 52, 133—Sam Zaslavsky.

Figure credits: Figs. 61a and b reprinted by permission of Claudia Zaslavsky: *The Multicultural Math Classroom: Bringing in the World* (Heinemann, A Division of Reed Elsevier, Inc., Portsmouth, NH, 1996). Figs. 43b and 57a, b, and c courtesy of J. Weston Walch, reprinted from *Multicultural Mathematics* by Claudia Zaslavsky. Copyright 1987, 1993.

First Edition
Published by Chicago Review Press, Incorporated
814 North Franklin Street
Chicago, Illinois 60610
ISBN 978-1-55652-287-1
Printed in the United States of America
10 9

This book is dedicated to all the children of the world.
May they have a bright future and enjoy peaceful games.

ACKNOWLEDGMENTS

I want to thank the many educators who shared their expertise to make this book possible. In particular, Judith Hankes contributed her material about the dream catcher; Esther Ilutsik shared her knowledge of Yup'ik border patterns; Marcia Ascher set me straight on the solution to the river-crossing puzzle involving the jealous husbands; and Beverly Ferrucci shared Japanese paper-cutting and several games. I am grateful to the authors of the many books listed in the Bibliography that were a source of information and inspiration for this collection. Cynthia Sherry was a most concerned and involved editor; she played all the games and carried out the activities, pointing out my mistakes and occasional lack of clarity. I take full responsibility for any remaining errors.

Table of Contents

Introduction

Did you know that some of the games that kids play were invented hundreds, even thousands, of years ago? Today you can play computer versions of Tic-tac-toe and Oware, games that go back at least 3,300 years to ancient Egypt.

The games, puzzles, and projects in this book come from all parts of the world—Africa, Asia, Europe, North America, and the island nations of Hawaii, the Philippines, and New Zealand (called Aotearoa by the Maori people who first lived there). These activities will introduce you to the people who played the games, who solved the puzzles, and who designed the art.

You will exercise your brain as you solve puzzles like the African children's network that a European scientist said was "impossible." You will follow the lead of Islamic artists who made beautiful patterns using only a compass and a straightedge (unmarked ruler). You will design and decorate game boards and make the game pieces you will need to play some of the games. You will make models of the homes that different people around the world live in.

In all of these activities you will be using math. Many of these math ideas are probably different from the math you learn in school. If a puzzle or activity doesn't work out at first, just keep trying. Read the hints and suggestions carefully. You might want to discuss the problem with a friend, teacher, or family member. Two heads are better than one!

Most of the activities are self-checking—you will know whether they are correct. See Chapter 10 for the answers to some of these activities, but you probably won't need them. It's much more satisfying to work out the solution yourself, even if it takes a while.

In this book you will read about two types of games for two or more people—games of strategy and games of chance. Some games require a game board and certain types of playing pieces or counters. Players must decide how they are going to move their pieces on the board. These are called games of strategy. Another kind of game depends upon the way the pieces fall. The players have no control over the outcome of the game, and such games are called games of chance.

It is interesting to see how a game changes as it travels from one place to another and is passed along from ancient times to the present. Three-in-a-row games and mankala games are good examples. You will learn several versions of each of these games.

The games of strategy require several types of game boards. Although you can draw them on paper, you will probably want boards that last for a while. Use sections of cardboard or mat board, and draw the lines neatly with the help of a ruler. It's a good idea to make a pattern on a sheet of scratch paper first. Be sure you measure carefully.

Many of these games call for two kinds of counters or markers. Kings and princes used to play with beautiful pieces made of gold and ivory. Ordinary people used pebbles, seeds, or bits of twig, peeled and unpeeled. You can use red and black checkers or two kinds of coins, beans, or buttons. Or you might like to make your own special counters.

Most of the games of strategy are for two players or two teams. You can also play them by yourself. Pretend that you are two people, and play on both sides of the board. This is a good way to learn a new game or to work out the fine points of strategy, as though you were solving a puzzle.

Some people play games just to win and get upset when they lose. Playing a game should be fun. When one player always wins, the other player must always lose and may give up after a while. Helping an opponent to improve his or her skills makes the game more interesting for both players.

In traditional games of strategy for two players, one side wins and the other side loses. Each player should have an equal chance of winning. In some games the first player to move is more likely to win. Players should take turns going first in this type of game. Perhaps you can figure out changes in the rules so that both players are winners. Cooperation may be more rewarding than competition.

You may want to vary the games. A slight change in the rules, or in the shape of the game board, or in the number of counters may call for an entirely different strategy. Just be sure that both players agree on the new rules before the game starts.

Most important—have fun!

Math Games & Activities from around the World

Figure 0

1

Three-in-a-Row Games

All over the world children play some form of a three-in-a-row game for two players. Tic-tac-toe is one example of such a game. The object of the game is to be the first player to get three markers in a row on the game board. It seems that people were playing such games long before the time of your great grandparents.

More than one hundred years ago, scientists examining the rooftop of an ancient Egyptian temple found several strange diagrams carved in the sandstone slabs. They looked like this: **Figure 0**

It turned out that every one of these diagrams is used as a game board for a three-in-a-row game somewhere in the world! Did the ancient Egyptians really play such games? How could the scientists find out?

The temple was built 3,300 years ago to memorialize the king, Pharaoh Seti I. It stands in the town of Qurna. Royal tombs were built on the west side of the Nile River. This was where the setting sun entered the spirit world for the night, according to Egyptian beliefs. Ancient Egyptians believed that people would have a life after death and would need all the things that they enjoyed while they were alive. So the tombs contain many items that were important to them in life, like clothing, jewelry, tools, and even their pets!

The Egyptians painted the walls of their tombs and temples with the scenes from the lives of their kings and queens and other wealthy people. Game boards and carved game pieces for Senet and other games were buried with the mummies of important Egyptians. That's how we know about the games that these people played when they were alive. But no game boards for three-in-a-row games have been found inside the tombs, and no pictures of people playing such games appear on temple walls.

How did these diagrams come to be on the roof of the Pharaoh's temple? Probably the workmen who built the temple played three-in-a-row games on the stone slabs during their lunch break. Instead of drawing a fresh game board in the sand for each game, they carved permanent diagrams in stone.

You may wonder whether Egyptian children played these games. Perhaps fathers played such games with their children at home. But they probably drew game boards in the dirt outside the house and wiped them away when the game was over, leaving no trace.

From Egypt the games could easily have spread all over the world. Greek scholars traveled to Egypt for higher education, just as people nowadays go to college. The Romans, who probably learned the games from the Greeks, spread them when they conquered parts of Europe, the Middle East, and North Africa. By that time the Chinese had already been playing three-in-a-row games for centuries. Game diagrams carved on the tops of stone walls and the steps of important buildings can still be found in many parts of the world.

The first European picture of children playing a three-in-a-row game appeared in Spain more than seven hundred years ago in the *Book of Games*. In the picture two children sit on either side of a large board for a game called Alquerque de Tres. The Spanish name means "mill with three." The game board they used is just like the board for Tapatan (see page 6).

Arabic-speaking Moors came to Spain from North Africa in the eighth century. They taught the Spanish people how to play games like Chess and Alquerque. Later the Spanish king Alfonso the Wise had this information written down in the *Book of Games*. Soon these games spread to other parts of Europe and, later, to America.

Now you will have a chance to learn several three-in-a-row games that children play in other parts of the world. As you will see, some of these games are more complicated than Tic-tac-toe. But the object of the game is always the same—to be the first player to get three markers in a row.

MAKE A MILL

Three-in-a-row games are called "mill" in many European countries. In England they are often referred to as "Morris," with a number telling how many counters each player uses. The word *Morris* may have come from the word *Moor,* the name of the people who brought the game to Europe by way of Spain.

Children in the United States play a three-in-a-row game called Tic-tac-toe. If you don't already know the game, you might ask a friend or an older person to teach it to you. In England they call the same game Noughts and Crosses. A nought is a zero, or 0, and a cross is an X. The players take turns marking X or 0 in the nine spaces of the game board.

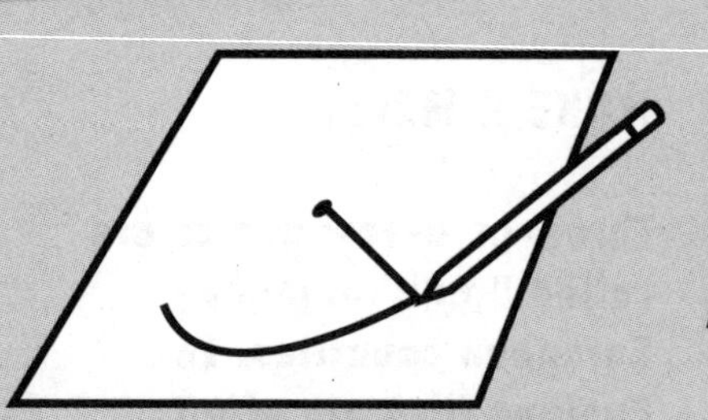

Figure 1a

Figure 1b

Shisima from Kenya

TWO PLAYERS

Kenya is a country in East Africa. Children in western Kenya play a three-in-a-row game called Shisima (Shi-SEE-Mah). The word *shisima* means "body of water" in the Tiriki language. They call the counters *imbalavali* or water bugs. Water bugs move so rapidly through the water that it is hard to keep them in sight. That's how quickly players of Shisima move their counters on the game board.

Children in Kenya draw the game board in the sand and play with bottle caps, pebbles, or buttons. You might also use coins. Just be sure that you can tell the difference between your counters and the other player's counters.

MATERIALS

- **Sheet of unlined paper, at least 8 inches (20cm) square**
- **Pencil with eraser**
- **Compass, or about 10 inches (25cm) of string**
- **Ruler**
- **Scissors**
- **Glue**
- **Piece of cardboard, at least 9 inches (22.5cm) square**
- **Colored markers or crayons**
- **3 counters for each player, of 2 different kinds (buttons, bottle caps, or coins)**

DRAWING THE GAME BOARD

The game board has the shape of an octagon (eight-sided polygon).

1. Mark the center of the paper. Use a compass to draw a large circle. If you don't have a compass, attach a piece of string to a pencil. Hold the pencil upright near the edge of the paper. Extend the string to the center and hold it down there. Then draw the circle. **Figure 1a**
2. Draw a line, called the diameter, through the center of the circle.

3. Draw another diameter, so that the two lines form a cross. These two lines are perpendicular to each other.
4. Draw two more diameters, each halfway between the first two.
5. Connect the endpoints of the diameters with straight lines to form an octagon. Erase the circle. **Figure 1b**
6. Draw the *shisima*, or body of water, in the center. Erase the lines in the center.
7. Glue your game board to the cardboard and decorate with colored markers. You might want to draw a border around your game board.

PLAYING THE GAME

Place the counters on the board, as shown in the diagram. **Figure 1c**

Players take turns moving their counters one space along a line to the next empty point. They continue to take turns moving one counter at a time. A player may move into the center, the *shisima*, at any time. Jumping over a counter is not allowed.

Each player tries to make a row with his or her three counters. A row must go through the *shisima*. There are four different ways to make a row. This diagram shows three black counters in a row. **Figure 1d**

The first player to get all three counters in a row is the winner. If the same set of moves is repeated three times, the game ends in a draw—no winner or loser. It's time to start a new game. Take turns being Player One.

After a few games you may be able to move your counters as fast as the *imbalavali* swim in the water.

THINGS TO THINK ABOUT

Is it a good idea to move into the *shisima* on your first move? Why or why not?

If each player has four counters, can they still play the game? Try it and see what happens.

Figure 1c

Figure 1d

Tapatan from the Philippines

TWO PLAYERS

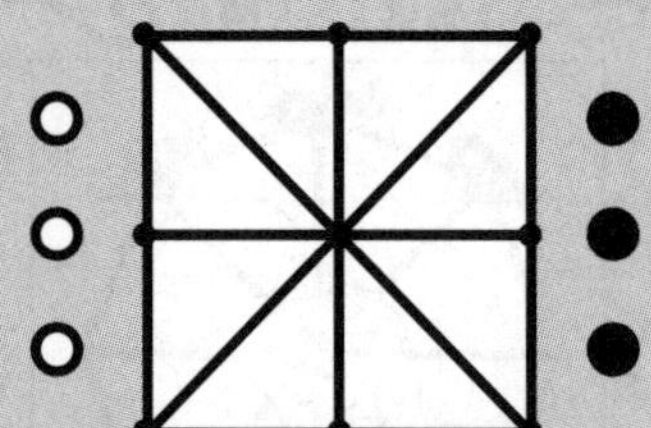

Figure 2a

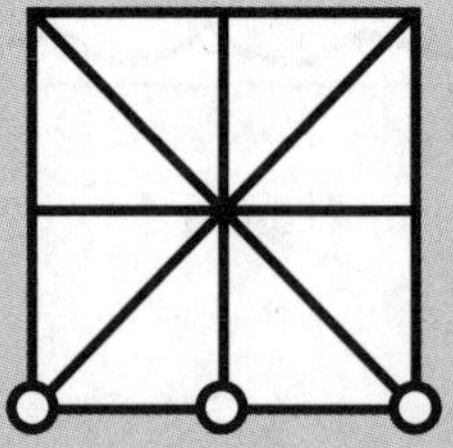

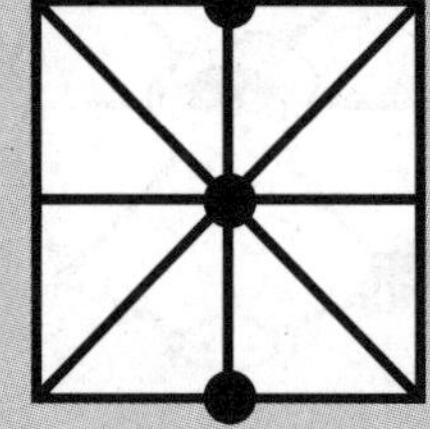

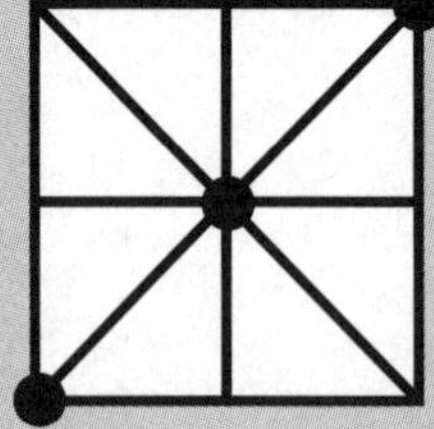

Figure 2b

Tapatan (TAP-uh-tan) is a game that people play in the Philippines, a country of many islands off the southeast coast of the Asian continent. Some families keep beautiful wooden game boards for Tapatan. Other families have the diagrams marked on floors or on doorsteps of their homes. They use special round counters for this game, three of light wood for one player and three of dark wood for the other.

MATERIALS

- **Sheet of unlined paper, at least 8 inches (20cm) square**
- **Pencil**
- **Ruler**
- **Colored markers or crayons**
- **Scissors**
- **Glue**
- **Piece of cardboard, at least 9 inches (22.5cm) square**
- **3 counters for each player, 3 light and 3 dark (beans, buttons, or coins)**

DRAWING THE GAME BOARD

1. Draw a square that measures six inches (15cm) on each side.
2. With your pencil, draw the diagonals.
3. Draw lines that connect the midpoints of the opposite sides.
4. Use a marker or crayon to mark the nine points where the lines meet as shown in the diagram. **Figure 2a**
5. Glue the paper to the cardboard and decorate your game board.

PLAYING THE GAME

This game is played on the nine points where the lines intersect. Players take turns going first. Player One places a light counter on any point. Then Player Two places a dark counter on any empty point. They take turns until all the counters have been placed on the game board.

Then Player One moves one of her counters along a line to the next empty point. Jumping over a counter is not allowed. Player Two does the same with one of his counters. They continue this way taking turns.

Each player tries to make a row of three counters of one color and block the other player from doing the same. A row can be made in eight different ways: three across, three down, and two along the diagonal. **Figure 2b**

The winner is the first player to make a row. If neither player can get three in a row and the same set of moves is repeated three times, the game ends in a draw—no winner or loser.

THINGS TO THINK ABOUT

Where should Player One place the first counter in order to win?

Can you play the game with four counters for each player?

How is Tapatan like Tic-tac-toe? How is it different?

Player One can place the first counter on any one of the nine points on the board. Show that there are really only three different ways to place the first counter: center, corner, and side. **Figure 2c**

CHANGING THE RULES

Children and grown-ups play games similar to Tapatan in many parts of the world, but the rules may be somewhat different. Here are some other versions of the game you might want to try:

Marelle (France). Neither player may make the first move in the center.

Achi (Ghana and Nigeria). Each player may have four counters instead of three.

Tant Fant (India). The game opens with each player's three counters already in position, as in this diagram. In Tant Fant, a row may not be made on the starting lines. There are just six different ways to make a row in this version. **Figure 2d**

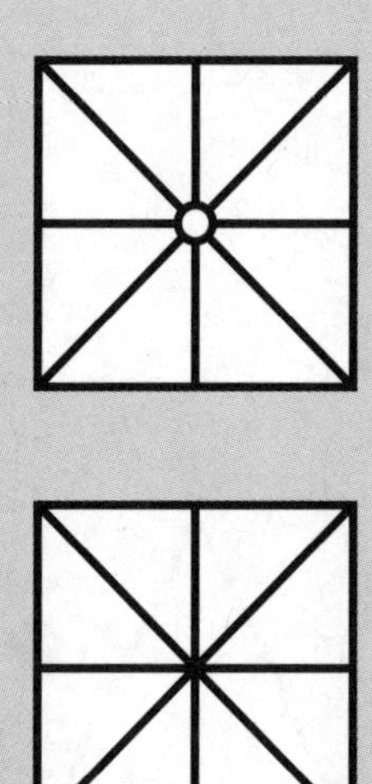

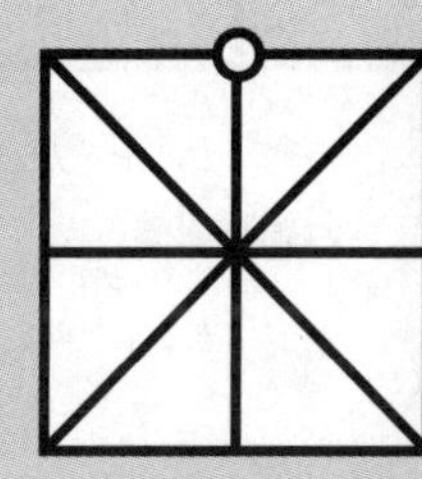

Figure 2c

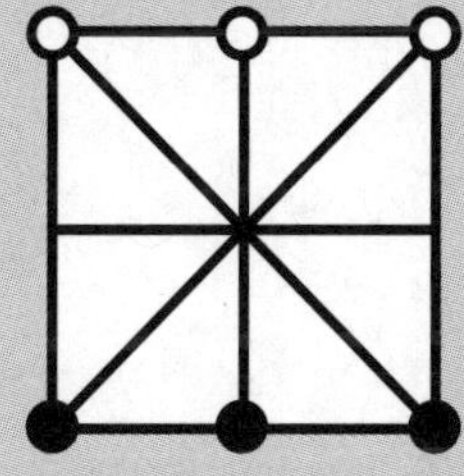

Figure 2d

Tsoro Yematatu from Zimbabwe

TWO PLAYERS

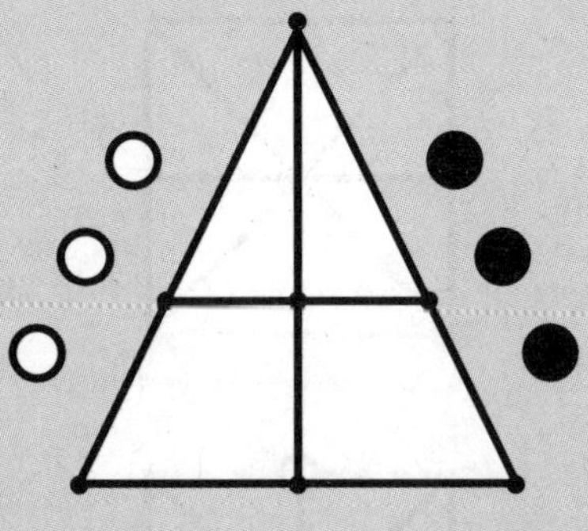

Figure 3

Zimbabwe is a country in southern Africa. It is named after the complex of buildings called Great Zimbabwe, or the "Great Stone House." In these buildings once lived the rulers of a vast ancient kingdom known for its rich gold mines.

Children in Zimbabwe play Tsoro Yematatu (TSOH-roh Yeh-mah-TAH-too), the "stone game played with three." Today they are most likely to use bottle caps as counters, as soft drinks are just as popular in Africa as they are in the United States.

MATERIALS

- **Sheet of unlined paper, at least 8 inches (20cm) square**
- **Pencil**
- **Ruler**
- **Colored markers or crayons**
- **Scissors**
- **Glue**
- **Sheet of cardboard, slightly larger than the paper**
- **3 counters for each player, of 2 different kinds (coins, buttons, or bottle caps)**

DRAWING THE GAME BOARD

1. The game board is in the shape of an isosceles triangle (it has two equal sides). With a pencil and ruler, draw a triangle on your sheet of paper as shown in the diagram. **Figure 3**
2. Draw an altitude that divides the triangle in half. Then connect the midpoints of the equal sides.
3. Go over your lines with a marker and mark the seven points where the lines intersect.
4. Glue the paper to the piece of cardboard. You may want to decorate the game board and keep it to use again.

PLAYING THE GAME

Players take turns placing their counters on the empty points of the board. After all the counters have been placed on the board, one empty point remains. Then each player in turn moves one of his or her counters to the empty point on the board. Jumping over a counter is allowed.

Each player tries to make a row of three. There are five different ways to do this. The winner is the first to make a row of three. This game can go on for a long time without a winner. In that case, the players should decide to call it a draw.

THINGS TO THINK ABOUT

Why can't you play the game with four counters for each player?

Picaría Native American

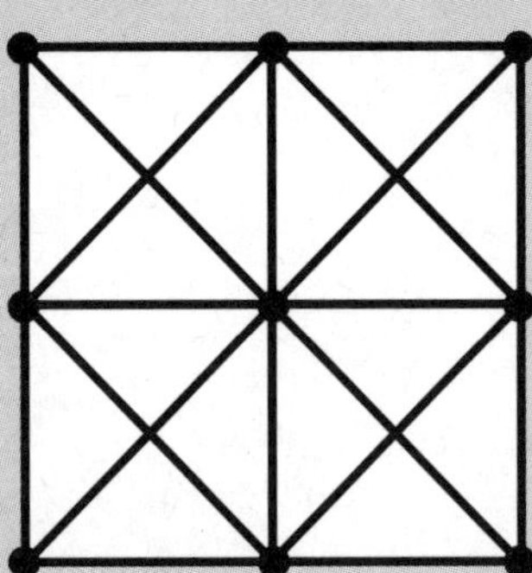

Figure 4a

Figure 4b

The Pueblo Indians of New Mexico play three-in-a-row games similar to those found halfway around the world. Did they make up these games themselves, or did they learn them from other people?

One clue is the name of the game. Some of the Pueblo people called their games Pitarilla or Picaría (Pick-ah-REE-ah). These words sound like the Spanish name for the game Pedreria, which means "little stone." Most likely the Native Americans of the Southwest learned the games from the Spanish.

In the sixteenth century, the Spanish conquistadores sailed from Spain to America searching for riches. They had heard that some towns in the Southwest were filled with gold. They attacked the towns but found no gold.

The Spanish conquistadores gave the name Pueblo to the people of this region. In Spanish, *pueblo* means both "people" and "town." The Spanish forced the Pueblo Indians to work like slaves. In 1680 the Pueblos revolted but were free from slavery for only twelve years. Imagine how much the Native Americans must have disliked their Spanish conquerors, and yet they continued to play the games they learned from them.

Pueblo children scratch their game boards on flat stones. For counters they use pebbles, dried corn kernels, or bits of pottery.

MATERIALS

- **Sheet of unlined paper, at least 8 inches (20cm) square**
- **Pencil**
- **Ruler**
- **Colored markers or crayons**
- **Scissors**
- **Glue**
- **Piece of cardboard, at least 9 inches (22.5cm) square**
- **3 counters for each player, of 2 different kinds (pebbles, coins, or bottle caps)**

DRAWING THE GAME BOARD

1. Draw a square that measures six inches (15cm) on each side.
2. Using your pencil, connect the midpoints of the opposite sides to form four small squares.
3. Then draw the diagonals of each of the four smaller squares. **Figure 4a**
4. Go over the lines with a marker. Mark the nine points on which the game is played—one in the center and eight along the sides, as shown in the diagram.
5. Glue the game board to the cardboard and decorate with markers or crayons. You may want to try a border design like these from Pueblo Indian artwork. **Figure 4b**

PLAYING THE GAME

The two players take turns placing one counter at a time on an empty point on the board. When all six counters have been placed, the players take turns moving one counter at a time along any line to the next empty point. Jumping over a counter is not allowed.

Each player tries to make a row with his or her three counters. A row can be made across, up and down, or along a diagonal—eight ways altogether.

The winner is the first player to make a row. If neither player can get three in a row, call it a draw and start again.

CHANGING THE RULES

Some people play Picaría on the thirteen points where the lines intersect, as shown in the diagram. **Figure 4c** Try playing on thirteen points by the game rules just given, with these differences:

1. Neither player may place a counter in the center of the board until all six counters are on the board.
2. Players may make three in a row, with no empty points between, anywhere along a diagonal. There are sixteen different ways to make three in a row.

THINGS TO THINK ABOUT

Which form of Picaría is a better game? Why?

Can you play the first version of Picaría with four counters for each player instead of three? How about the second version of the game?

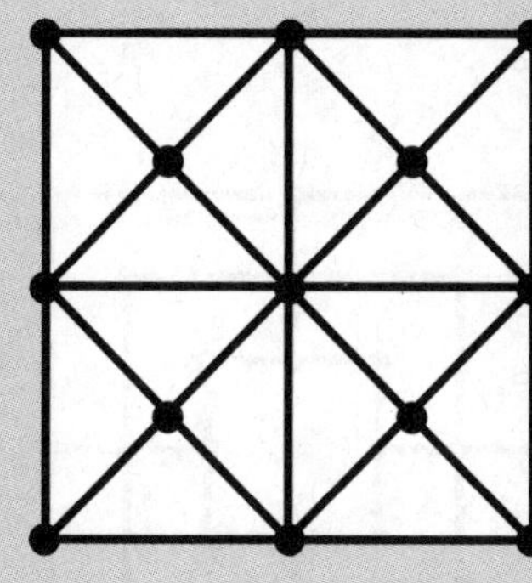

Figure 4c

9 Men's Morris from England

TWO PLAYERS

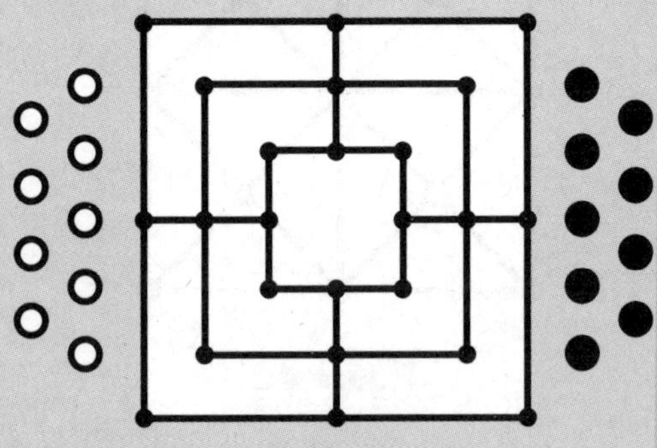

Figure 5a

For hundreds of years people in England have played three-in-a-row games. Some had names like Three Men's Morris, Five Men's Morris, Nine Men's Morris, and Twelve Men's Morris. The number told you how many counters each player used in the game.

English pageants during the Renaissance used girls and boys as counters in Nine Men's Morris. Imagine the scene as men in red velvet and women in lace-trimmed gowns gathered around the large Morris diagram marked in the earth. They watched as game masters ordered their living game pieces to move along the lines of the squares and would call out "Good Move!" or "Watch Out!"

Although Morris games have been popular in England for centuries, the game itself goes back thousands of years. A thousand-year-old burial ship of a Viking prince was dug up in Gokstad, Norway, and among its possessions was a wooden game board of three connected squares. The ship's sailors had cut the same diagram in the wooden planks of the deck for their own games. It is likely that the Vikings from Scandinavia learned the game and spread it around the world when they sailed to other parts of Europe, northern Africa, Asia, and even America.

Norwegians still use this same board today for the game they call Mølle. Germans call the same game Mühle, Russians call it Melnitsa, in Hungary it is Malom, and in Italy it is called Mulinello. All these names mean "mill." In Nigeria a similar game is known as Akidada, and in Arabic-speaking countries the game is called Dris.

MATERIALS

- **Pencil**
- **Ruler**
- **Sheet of unlined paper, at least 8 inches (20cm) square**
- **Colored markers or crayons**
- **Glue**
- **Piece of cardboard, at least 9 inches (22.5cm) square**
- **9 counters for each player, of 2 different kinds (beans, buttons, or coins)**

DRAWING THE GAME BOARD

1. Using your pencil and ruler, draw three squares one inside the other on your paper. Plan and measure carefully, so that the board fits on the paper and there is enough room to move the counters.
2. Draw four lines connecting the midpoints of the sides, as shown in the diagram. **Figure 5a**
3. Go over the pencil lines with markers or crayons. Mark the twenty-four points where the lines intersect.
4. Then glue the paper to the cardboard. Decorate your game board with markers or crayons.

PLAYING THE GAME

The two players take turns placing one counter at a time on an empty point on the game board. When all eighteen counters have been placed, the players take turns moving one counter at a time along a line to the next empty point. Jumping over a counter is not allowed.

Each player tries to make a row of three counters of the same kind along any straight line. A row of three is called a "mill." There are sixteen different ways to make a mill. Can you find them?

Here are two ways to make a mill: **Figure 5b**

A player who makes a mill may remove one of the other player's counters from the board, with one exception. You may not remove a counter from the other player's mill unless no other counter of that kind is on the board. Counters that have been removed from the board are out of the game.

The loser is the player who has only two counters left on the board or who is blocked from moving.

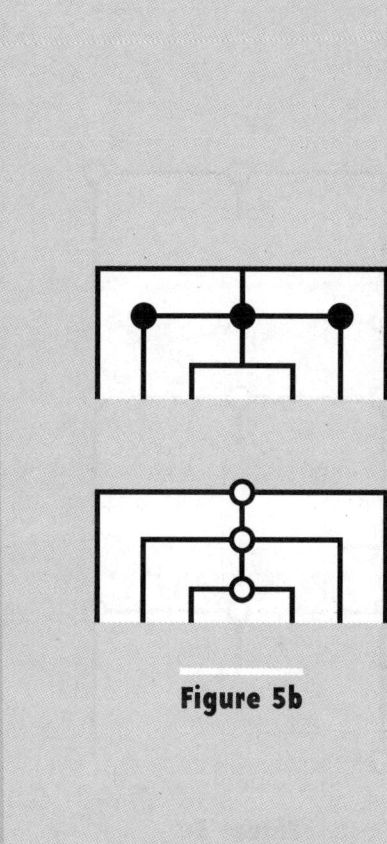

Figure 5b

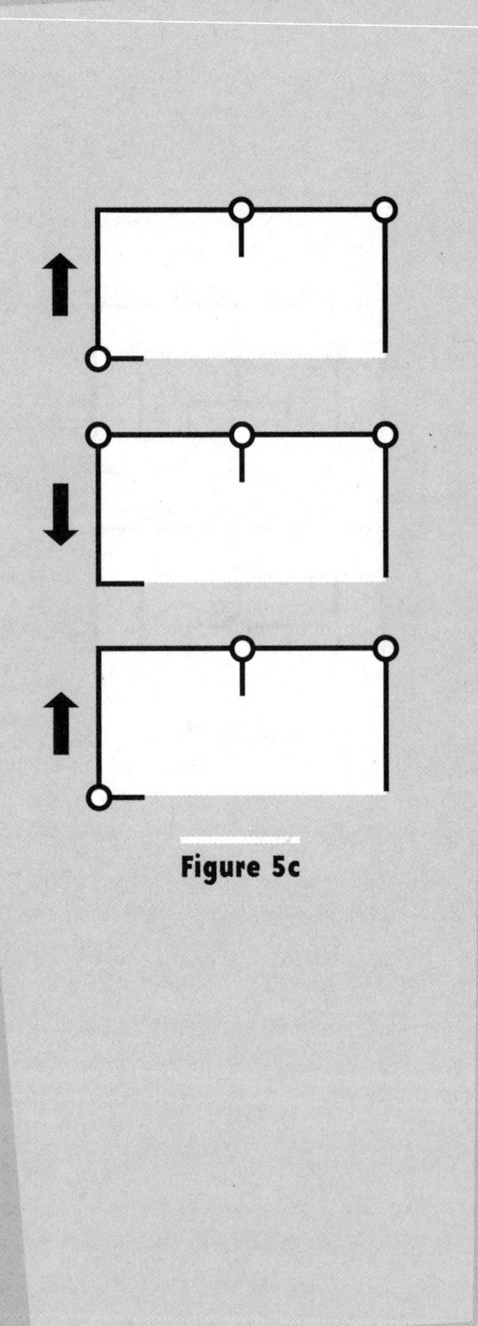
Figure 5c

HOW TO BE A GOOD PLAYER

It is a good strategy to spread your counters out on the board. This will make it harder for the other player to block you. Don't try to make a mill while you are placing your counters on the board.

When you put your counters on the board, place them so that you will be able to move each counter in more than one direction.

Move your counters so that you will have a choice of more than one way to form a mill on a future move.

Position three counters so that you can move one back and forth to close and then open a mill. Every time you close a mill, you capture one of the other player's counters. **Figure 5c**

THINGS TO THINK ABOUT

Can you think of a plan that will always work so that you can close and open a mill many times? Can you work out a strategy to block the other player from using an "open and close" plan to make more than one mill? What other strategies can you figure out?

CHANGING THE RULES

Have a rule that the same counter may not be moved twice in two successive moves.

In a version called Going Wild, a player who has only three counters left on the board may move them, one at a time, to any empty point on the board.

Trique from Colombia

TWO PLAYERS

Children in Colombia, a country in South America, play a three-in-a-row game that they call Trique (TREE-keh). A player who makes a row of three calls out "Trique," the Spanish word for a clever trick.

MATERIALS

- **Pencil**
- **Ruler**
- **Sheet of unlined paper, at least 8 inches (20cm) square**
- **Colored markers or crayons**
- **Glue**
- **Piece of cardboard, at least 9 inches (22.5cm) square**
- **9 counters for each player, of 2 different kinds (beans, coins, or buttons)**

DRAWING THE GAME BOARD

1. Using your pencil and ruler, draw three squares on the sheet of paper, one inside the other, as shown in the diagram. **Figure 6**
2. Then draw four lines connecting the midpoints of the sides of the squares, and four more lines connecting the corners of the squares. Plan your layout carefully so that you have enough space to move the counters.
3. Go over the lines with markers or crayons and mark the twenty-four points where the lines intersect.
4. Glue the sheet of paper to the cardboard. If you already have a board for Nine Men's Morris (page 12), all you need to do is add four lines connecting the corners of the squares. Decorate your game board with markers or crayons.

PLAYING THE GAME

Follow the rules for Nine Men's Morris (page 12), with one exception. In Trique, you may move your counters and make rows of three along the diagonal lines connecting the corners. Find the twenty different ways to make a row of three.

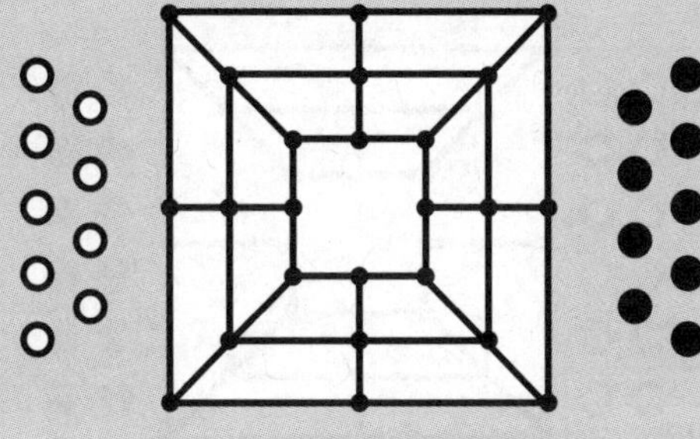

Figure 6

Nerenchi from Sri Lanka

TWO PLAYERS OR TWO TEAMS

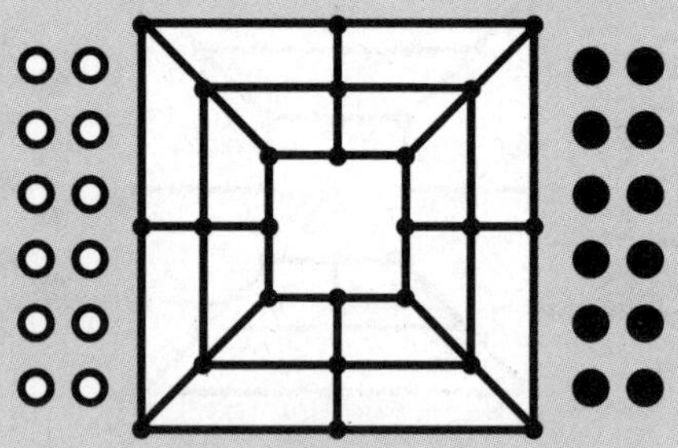

Figure 7a

Nerenchi is an ancient three-in-a-row game played in the Asian country of Sri Lanka. Diagrams for such games were carved in temple steps about two thousand years ago. Nerenchi has long been a special favorite of women and girls in Sri Lanka. They often play in teams, with the members of each team taking turns.

MATERIALS

- **Sheet of unlined paper, at least 8 inches (20cm) square**
- **Ruler**
- **Pencil**
- **Colored markers or crayons**
- **Glue**
- **Piece of cardboard or construction paper, at least 9 inches (22.5cm) square**
- **12 counters for each player or team, of 2 different kinds (beans, buttons, or coins)**

DRAWING THE GAME BOARD

The game board for Nerenchi is exactly like the board for Trique (page 15). **Figure 7a**

PLAYING THE GAME

The object of the game is to get a row of three counters, called a "nerenchi." The row can be made along the side of a square, along a line joining the midpoints of the sides of the squares, or along a diagonal line joining the corners. There are twenty ways to make a nerenchi.

Here are three different ways to make a nerenchi: **Figure 7b**

To Begin. The players, or teams, take turns placing one counter at a time on an empty point on the board. This part of the game ends when twenty-two counters are on the board, leaving two empty points. The remaining two counters may or may not be used in the game.

A player who makes a nerenchi during the "placing" stage of the game takes an extra turn, and he or she may do so for each nerenchi made. One player may have twelve counters on the board, while the other player may have only ten counters.

To Move. The last player to place a counter on the board makes the first move. The players, or teams, take turns moving one counter at a time along a line to the next empty point. You may not move along the diagonal lines, and you may not jump over a counter. Note that although you may not move your counters along a diagonal line, you are allowed to make a nerenchi along a diagonal line.

Each player or team tries to make as many nerenchis as possible. A player who makes a nerenchi during the "moving" stage of the game may remove one of the opponent's counters from any position on the board.

To Finish. The loser is the player or team that has lost all but two counters or is blocked from moving.

Children in southern Africa play Murabaraba, a three-in-a-row game with the same number of counters. The board is very much like the board for Nerenchi, and the rules are almost the same. A similar game called Twelve Men's Morris was popular in the New England colonies more than two hundred years ago. Other three-in-a-row games played with twelve counters for each player are: Sam K'i in China, Kon-tjil in Korea, Dig Dig in Malaysia, and Shah in Somalia.

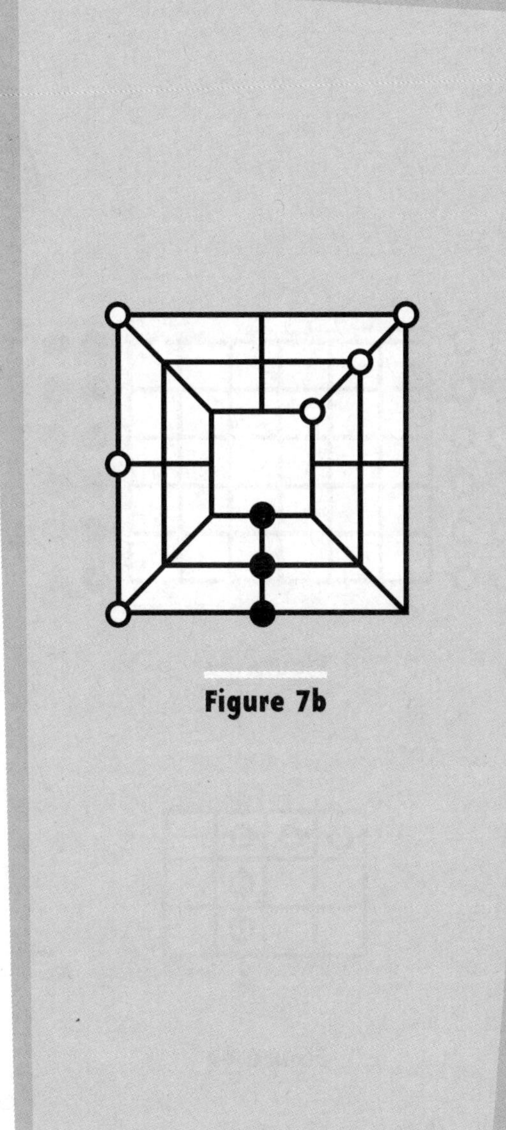

Figure 7b

Dara from Nigeria

TWO PLAYERS
OR
TWO TEAMS

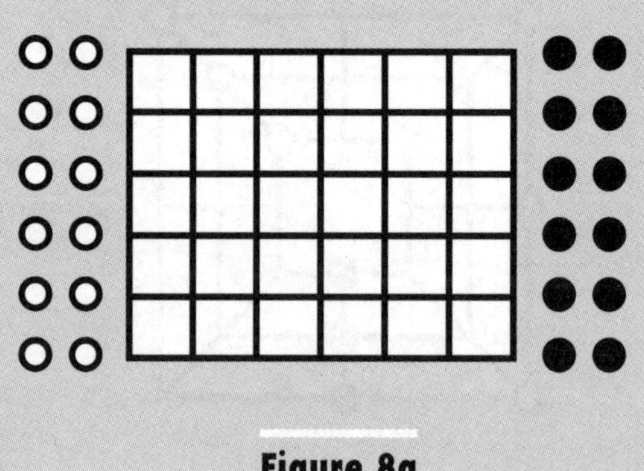

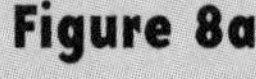

Figure 8a

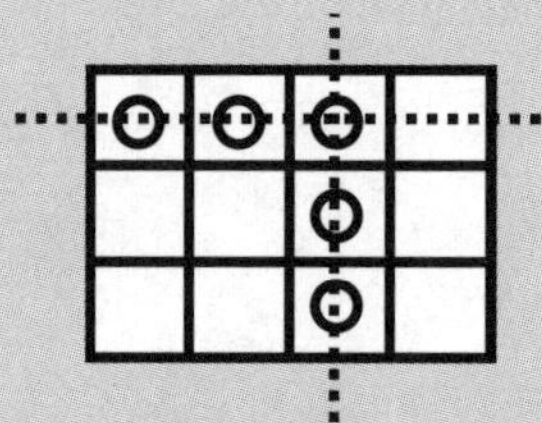

Figure 8b

This game for two players or two teams is popular among the men and boys in northern Nigeria, Niger, Mali, and other parts of northwestern Africa. They play the game with stones or sticks placed in holes dug in the earth or in the desert sand. You may play on a 5-row, 6-column board similar to part of a checkerboard.

Good Dara players are held in great honor. After the day's work is done, champions travel from village to village challenging local players. The contests may continue into the night for as long as the moon shines brightly. A champion will teach the game to his son as soon as the child is old enough to learn the rules. Later the father tells the boy the secrets of the game, secrets that he learned from his father or grandfather.

MATERIALS

- **Sheet of scratch paper**
- **Pencil**
- **Ruler**
- **Piece of construction paper or cardboard, at least 8 inches (20cm) square**
- **Marker**
- **12 counters for each player, of 2 different kinds (beans, buttons, or bottle caps)**

DRAWING THE GAME BOARD

1. Practice drawing your game board on scratch paper in pencil first. You need a rectangle divided into five rows of six squares each.
2. Then draw the game board on construction paper or cardboard. First use a ruler to measure carefully, and mark the main points in pencil. Then draw the lines. **Figure 8a**
3. Go over the lines with a marker.

PLAYING THE GAME

Two players, or teams, take turns placing one counter at a time inside any empty square, until all twenty-four counters have been placed. Then the players take turns moving one counter at a time to the next empty space. Moves may be made up, down, or sideways, but not diagonally. Jumping over a counter is not allowed.

Each player tries to get three counters in a row with no spaces between them. A row can be either across or up and down. A player who makes a row may remove one of the opponent's counters from the board. This is called "eating" the enemy, just as a lion eats its prey.

A player may not have more than three counters in a continuous line at any time.

A row made during the "placing" stage does not count. A player who makes two rows in one move may capture only one of the opponent's counters. See the diagram for an example. **Figure 8b**

The game ends when one player can no longer make a row. Then the opponent is the winner.

THINGS TO THINK ABOUT

Can you plan how to arrange five counters so that you can make a row on each move? This is called a "horse" and is a sure way to win. Here are two ways to do it. Can you find other ways? **Figure 8c**

CHANGING THE RULES

Some African players follow one or more of these rules for Dara:

Play on a checkerboard having six rows and six columns.

A counter may be captured from the opponent's row only if the opponent has no other counters on the board.

Neither player may remove a counter from a row. Therefore, the "horse" strategy cannot be used in this game. The player who makes three rows before the opponent makes one row wins the game.

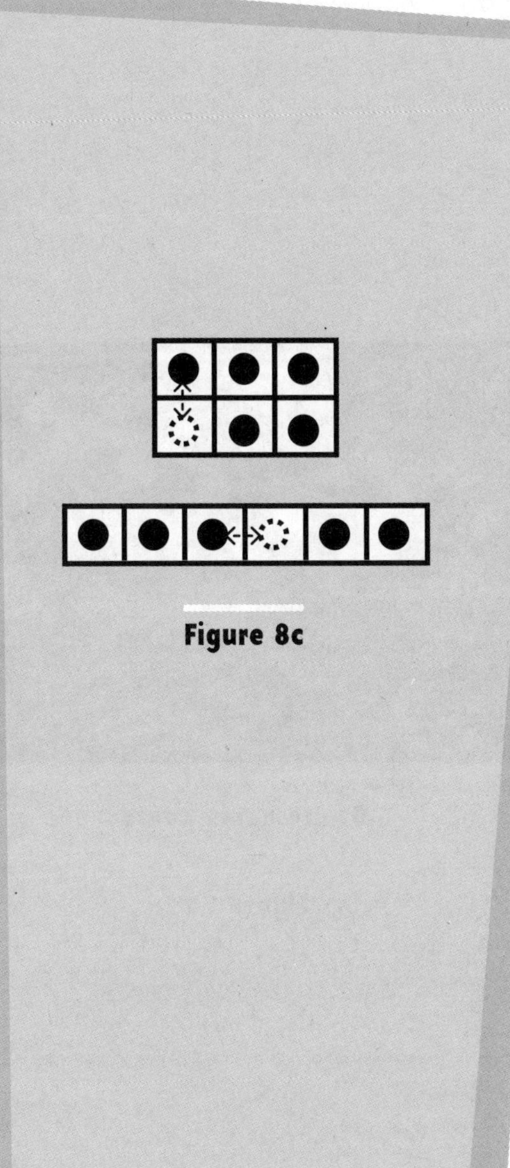

Figure 8c

2

Mankala: Board Games of Transfer

Oware game board

Figure 9a

Mankala is considered by game experts to be among the best games in the world. Mankala games are widespread. You will find them in most African countries, as well as in India, Indonesia, the Philippines, Sri Lanka, Central Asia, and Arabic countries. As captives in the horrendous slave trade, Africans brought the games to parts of the Americas—eastern Brazil, Suriname, and the Caribbean islands—where they are popular even today.

Games of this type are thousands of years old. Game boards were cut into the stones of several temples in ancient Egypt. Other very old rock-cut boards were discovered in Ghana, Uganda, and Zimbabwe.

The word *mankala* is Arabic for "transferring." Stones or seeds are transferred from one cup to another on a board having two, three, or four rows of cups. In each region the game has its own name and its own set of rules. The two-row board is popular in North Africa, West Africa, and parts of East Africa, under such names as Wari, Oware, Ayo, and Giuthi. People in Asia play Sungka, Dakon, and Congklak on two-row boards. In eastern and southern Africa the four-row board game is most common, with names like Bao (meaning "board" in Swahili), Nchuba, and Mweso. Ethiopia has three-row versions. **Figure 9a**

The game has been played by kings on beautiful carved wooden boards or boards of gold, and by children who scoop out holes in the ground. About four hundred years ago a king in central Africa, King Shyaam aMbul aNgoong, brought the game to his people, the Kuba, living in Congo. He induced them to give up warlike activities in favor of the peaceful arts. A statue of the king, now in the British Museum, shows him seated in front of a mankala game board.

When I was in Nigeria I watched as two teenaged carvers of game boards played each other. The seeds moved so fast around the board that I had no idea what the players were doing. In a few minutes, the game was over. They were experts because they had played the game since they were small children. Then one of the carvers offered to play a game with me. He showed me how to make each move so that I would win. Of course, I bought one of his game boards. The board had hinges in the middle so that you could close it up and keep the seeds inside. It made a fine game for travel. **Figure 9b**

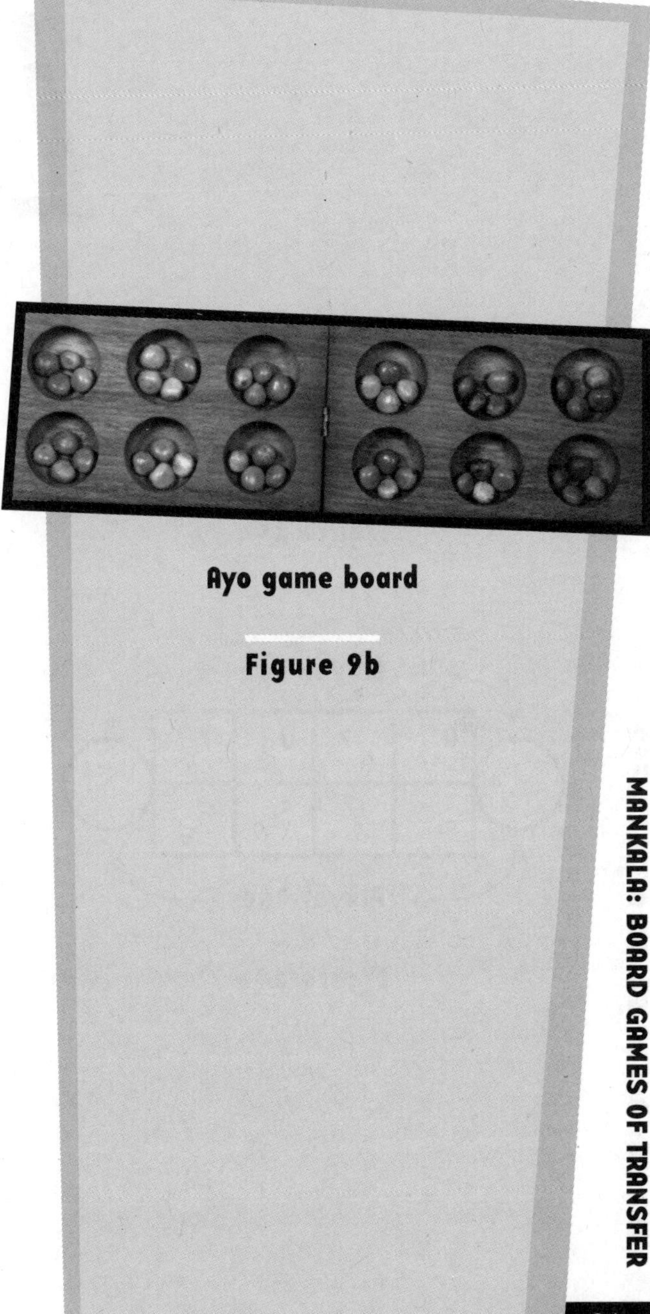

Ayo game board

Figure 9b

Easy Oware from Ghana

TWO PLAYERS

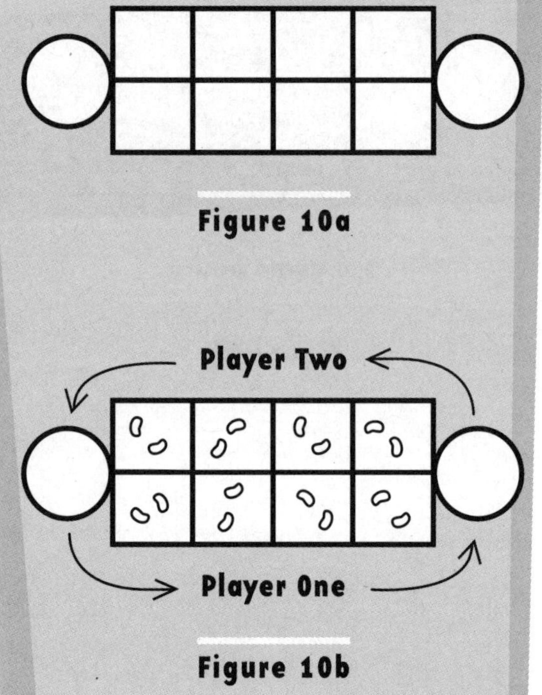

Figure 10a

Figure 10b

Asante people in Ghana, a country in West Africa, play the game called Oware (oh-WAHR-ee). Children and grown-ups alike enjoy the game. Two people face each other with the game board between them. Children often scoop out holes in the ground for their "board" and gather pebbles or large seeds to use as counters. The Yoruba people of southwest Nigeria play the same game, but they call it Ayo (EYE-oh). They use certain gray seeds as counters.

If you and your opponent have never played the game, you might want to start with this simple form. Playing on a flat sheet of paper helps you to see exactly what happens with each move. In the next section you can learn about the real Oware game.

MATERIALS

- **Sheet of unlined paper, at least 10 inches (25cm) long**
- **Ruler**
- **Pencil**
- **Marker**
- **2 small bowls or cups**
- **16 counters of 1 kind (beans, buttons, or shells)**

DRAWING THE GAME BOARD

1. Draw a game board in the shape of a large rectangle having two rows of four squares each. Each square should be large enough to hold several beans. Use a ruler and pencil and measure carefully. **Figure 10a**
2. Go over the lines with a marker.
3. Place one bowl or cup, called "endpot," at each end of the game board.

PLAYING THE GAME

The players sit facing each other with the game board between them. Place two beans or other counters in each space. The four spaces, called "cups," on each side of the board belong to the player nearest them. The endpot to the right of each player belongs to that player. **Figure 10b**

To Move. Player One picks up all the beans in any one of her cups and drops one bean into each cup, going to her right (counter-clockwise). This is called "sowing the seeds." Some beans may fall into the cups on Player Two's side of the board. **Figure 10c**

Then Player Two picks up all the beans in any one of his cups. He drops one bean in each cup going around the board to his right. The players take turns in this way. Do not "sow" into the endpots.

To Capture. Captures are made from the opponent's side of the board. If the last bean in any move makes a group of two in a cup on the opponent's side, the last player captures these two beans and places them into her endpot. Then, going backward, if the cup just before the previous one on the opponent's side also has two beans, the player may capture them and place them in her endpot. Continue to capture as long as each cup has just two beans and is on the far side of the board. **Figure 10d**

To Finish. The game ends when one person has no beans left on his or her side of the board. Then the beans in the endpots are counted, and the player who has captured more beans is the winner.

THINGS TO THINK ABOUT AND DO

Practice playing this game by yourself to learn how to make good moves. Practice different kinds of moves and see how many beans you can capture with each move.

Try playing with twenty-four beans. Start with three beans in each cup. How would you change the rule about captures?

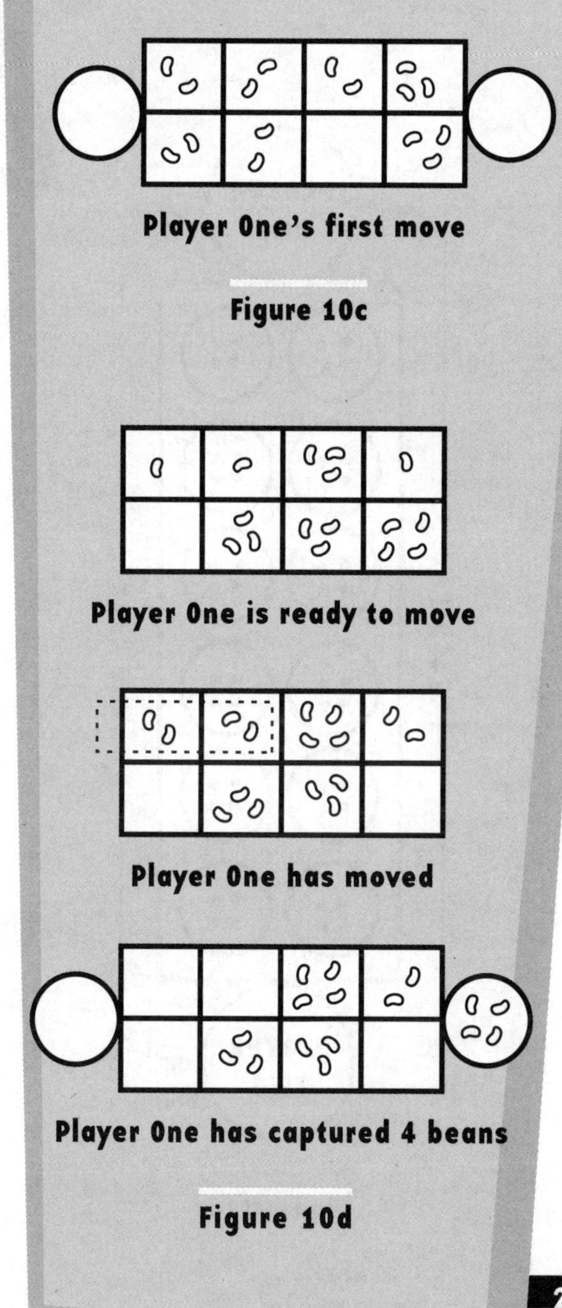

Figure 10c

Figure 10d

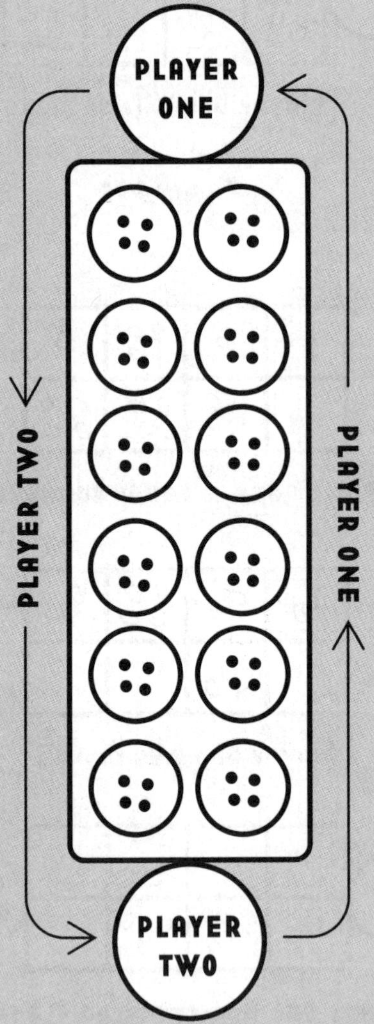

PLAYER ONE

PLAYER TWO

PLAYER ONE

PLAYER TWO

Figure 11a

The Real Oware Game from Ghana

TWO PLAYERS

Once you have practiced playing Easy Oware (page 22) try this version of the game, which is a bit more challenging, but lots of fun.

MATERIALS

- **Empty (one dozen) egg carton with the lid removed**
- **Colored markers**
- **2 small bowls or cups**
- **48 counters, of 1 kind (beans, buttons, or shells)**

MAKING THE GAME BOARD

The board has six cups on each side, twelve cups altogether. An egg carton makes a perfect game board. You might want to decorate it with African patterns and colors. Place one bowl or cup at each end of the board as an endpot to hold the captured beans. **Figure 11a**

PLAYING THE GAME

The players sit facing each other with the game board between them. Place four beans or other counters in each space. The six spaces, called "cups," on each side of the board belong to the player nearest them. The endpot to the right of each player belongs to that player.

To Move. As in Easy Oware players take turns picking up all the beans in any one of their cups and dropping them, one bean into each cup, going to their right (counterclockwise). This is called "sowing the seeds." Some beans may fall into the cups on the other player's side of the board. Do not "sow" into the endpots.

When players sow from a cup that has twelve or more beans, they must skip over the cup the beans came from and leave that cup empty, as they sow around the board.

To Capture. If the last bean dropped into a cup on the opponent's side of the board makes a group of two or three, those beans may be captured. Then, going backward, groups of two or three beans may be captured from cups that are next to each other on the far side of the board. **Figure 11b**

To Finish. If all the opponent's cups are empty, a player must move beans into them on his or her turn. If the player cannot do so, the game ends. The player adds the beans on his or her side to those in the endpot. Beans that go around and around with no captures may be divided equally between the players. The player with more beans in his or her endpot is the winner.

THINGS TO THINK ABOUT AND DO

Play both sides by yourself. Plan the best moves that will lead to capturing the opponent's beans.

When you are learning the game, you may want to place three beans in each cup, or thirty-six beans altogether. What other rules might you change? Perhaps you will invent a version of Oware that people already play in other parts of the world. The next few pages will describe some of these versions.

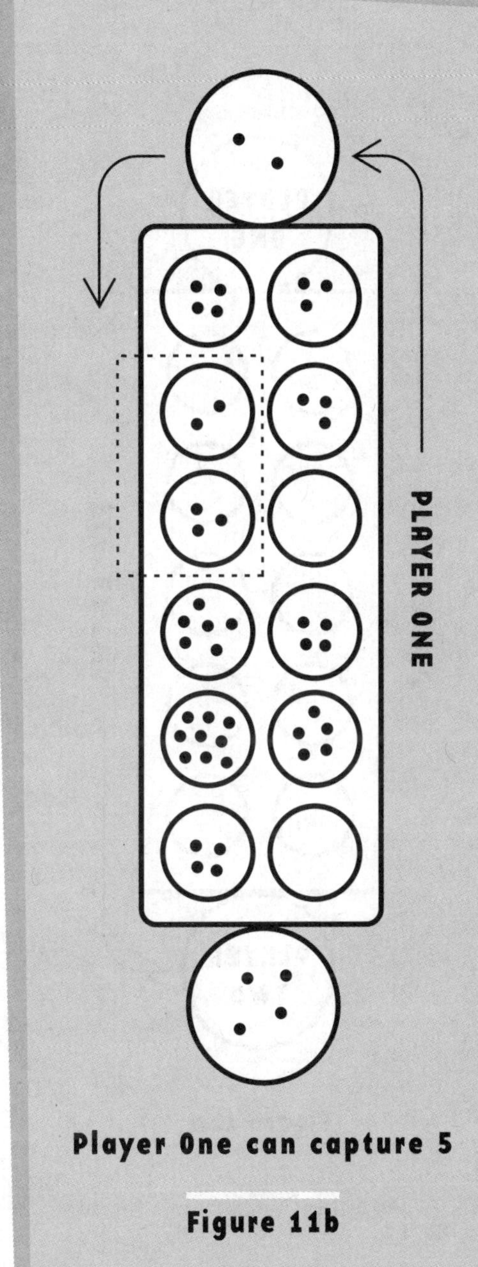

Player One can capture 5

Figure 11b

Sungka from the Philippines

TWO PLAYERS

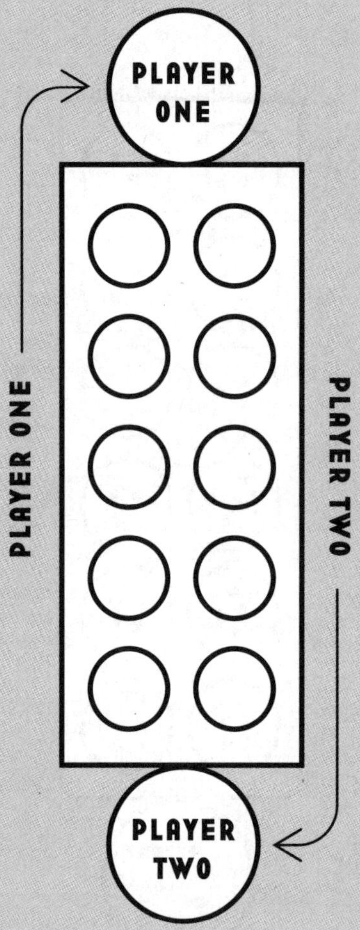

PLAYER ONE

PLAYER TWO

PLAYER ONE

PLAYER TWO

Figure 12a

Children in the Philippine Islands like to play a mankala-type game known as Sungka (Soon-KAH). Similar games are called Chonka in Malaysia and Congklak in Indonesia. A book editor who grew up in the Philippines told me that she had learned more math playing Sungka than she learned in school! She probably meant that she enjoyed the game more than she enjoyed schoolwork.

The rules for this game differ from those for Oware in several important respects:

1. All moves are *clockwise,* going to the player's left.
2. Players may make several laps in one move.
3. Players drop a counter into their own endpot as they go around the board.
4. Each player's endpot is to his or her left; and capturing is done differently.

MATERIALS

- **Empty (one dozen) egg carton with the lid removed**
- **Scissors**
- **1 or 2 small bowls or cups**
- **50 counters, of 1 kind (beans, shells, pebbles, or buttons)**

MAKING THE GAME BOARD

This game board has two rows of five cups and two endpots, one at each end. Using your scissors, cut the partition between two cups of the egg carton at one end, and use the spare as an endpot for captured beans. Place a bowl, or endpot, at the other end of the board to store captured beans. **Figure 12a**

PLAYING THE GAME

The fifty beans are distributed, five to a cup. Two players face each other with the game board between them. The five spaces, or cups, on each side belong to the player nearest them. The endpot to the left belongs to that player.

To Move. Players take turns picking up the beans from any of the cups on their side, and sowing them one-by-one into the cups going to their left (clockwise) around the board. Players drop one bean into their endpot as they go around the board, but not into the opponent's endpot.

If the last bean drops into a cup that already has beans, the player picks up all the beans in that cup and continues to sow in a clockwise direction.

If the last bean falls into an empty cup on the opponent's side or into their own storage cup, it is the opponent's turn to move.

To Capture. If the last bean falls into an empty cup on the player's side of the board and the cup opposite it has beans, the player may capture those beans and place them in his or her endpot. Then it is the opponent's turn. **Figure 12b**

To Finish. When there are no beans left on a player's side, the opponent adds the beans on his or her side to those in the endpot. The winner is the player with more beans in his or her endpot.

THINGS TO THINK ABOUT

How is Sungka similar to Oware? Can you play Sungka on an Oware board that has six cups in each row? How would you change the rules?

CHANGING THE RULES

People often play on a board that has two rows of seven cups and start by placing seven shells in each cup. How many shells are needed?

Player One moves 5 beans

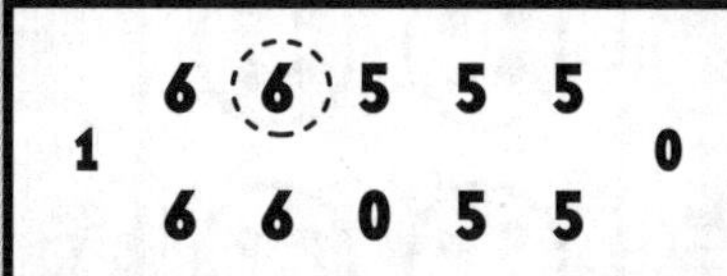

Player One continues, and drops 6 beans

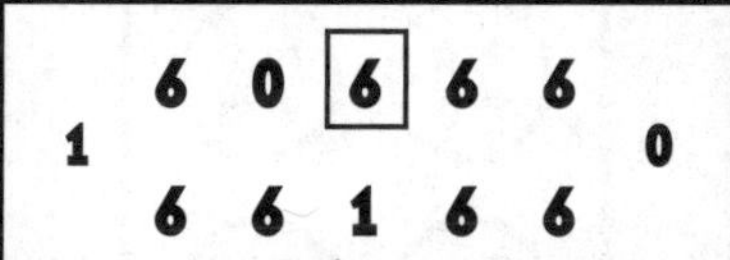

Player One captures 6 beans

Figure 12b

Giuthi from Kenya

TWO PLAYERS
OR
TWO TEAMS

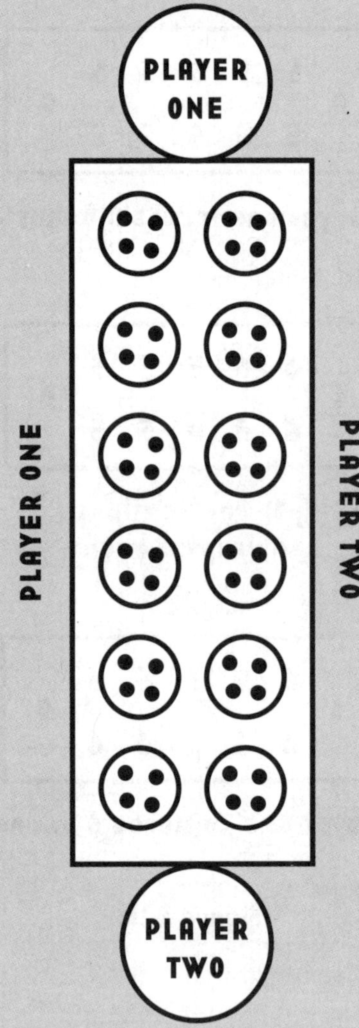

PLAYER ONE

PLAYER ONE

PLAYER TWO

PLAYER TWO

Figure 13a

The Kikuyu people of central Kenya play a version of mankala that they call Giuthi (Ghee-YOU-thee). The board has two rows of six cups. At each end is a storage cup for captured seeds. The Kikuyu have traditionally been breeders of cattle, and the words they use in the game reflect their occupation. The counters are referred to as "cattle in the fields," and the captured pieces are placed in "sheds." Most people play the game outdoors. Boys and girls often play the game as they look after their cattle and goats.

MATERIALS

- **Empty (one dozen) egg carton with the lid removed**
- **2 small bowls or cups for storage, called "sheds"**
- **48 counters, of 1 kind (beans, buttons, or shells)**

PLAYING THE GAME

Using the egg carton as a game board, the two players, or teams, face each other across the game board. Each player owns the six cups on his or her side of the board and the bowl or cup for storage at his or her right. The beans are distributed four to each cup. **Figure 13a**

To Move. Player One picks up all the beans in any cup on his or her side and drops them, one by one, in each cup going around the board. The player chooses the direction—either to the right (counterclockwise) or to the left (clockwise). The player picks up all the beans in the last cup he or she dropped a bean into and distributes them, one by one, in the opposite direction. Player One continues in this way, changing direction each time, until the last bean falls into an empty cup. Players do not drop beans into the storage cups.

If the last bean falls into an empty cup on the player's side, but he or she has not dropped any beans in the cups on the opponent's side, the player moves again. The Kikuyu say: "You can't steal the other person's cattle unless you cross into his land." That means you must drop beans in your opponent's cups before you may capture your opponent's beans.

If the last bean falls in an empty cup on the opponent's side of the board, it is the opponent's turn. The game continues in this way, unless a player captures the opponent's beans.

To begin any move, a player must pick up the beans in a cup that contains at least two beans.

To Capture. If, in the course of a move, Player One has dropped beans in the opponent's cups, and the last bean in Player One's hand falls into an empty cup on his or her own side, then Player One may capture all the beans in the opponent's cup opposite that cup (which now has one bean in it). If the cup next to this cup is also empty, Player One may capture beans in the opponent's cup opposite it. Player One continues to capture as long as there is an unbroken sequence of empty cups on his or her side in the direction he or she is moving. Capturing ends with an occupied cup on the player's side of the board or with an empty cup on the opponent's side of the board. **Figure 13b**

To FInish. The game is over when neither player can make a move according to the rules. Each player takes the "cattle" on his or her side of the board and adds them to those in the "shed." The player with more cattle is the winner.

THINGS TO THINK ABOUT

How is Giuthi similar to Oware? How is it different? How is Giuthi similar to Sungka? How is it different?

CHANGING THE RULES

The Kikuyu play with as many as nine beans in each cup. The board may have anywhere from five to ten cups in each of the two rows.

The rules given above are for the first stage of the game only. The second part is more complicated and is not included here.

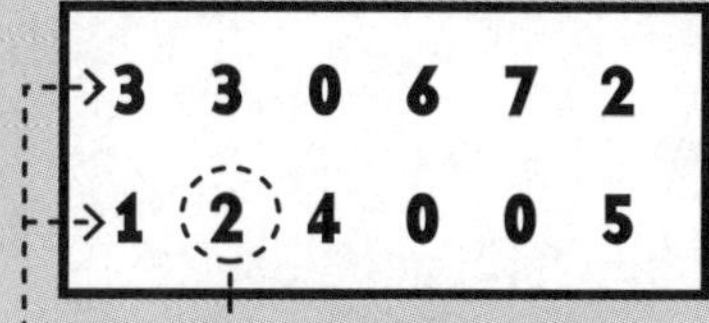

Player One moves 2 beans to the left

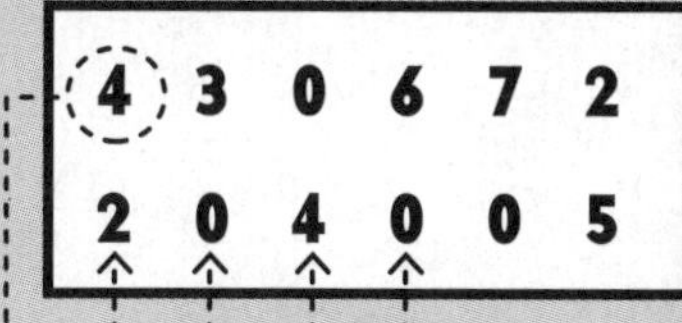

Player One moves 4 beans

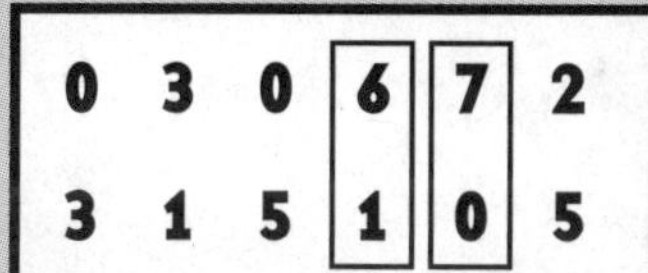

Player One captures 14 beans

Figure 13b
One move for Player One

3

More Board Games

In this section you will learn two blocking games and several games that are more or less like checkers. All but one of the games are for two players and involve moving the counters on a game board.

Pong Hau K'i, from China, and Mu Torere, a Maori game from New Zealand (the Maori call their land Aotearoa), are rather similar. We can think of Mu Torere as a more complex version of Pong Hau K'i, because it requires more counters and is played on a larger board. In both games the winner is the player who has blocked the opponent from making any moves.

A five-pointed star was one of the diagrams scratched into the roof stones at the ancient Egyptian temple to the king, Pharaoh Seti I, at Qurna about 3,300 years ago. Two games that use this diagram, called a pentagram, are Pentalpha, for one player, and Kaooa, for two players. Pentalpha is a Greek name for the game—really more like a puzzle—that is played on the Mediterranean island of Crete. Kaooa, also called Vultures and Crows, is popular in India.

Awithlaknannai is based on the Arabic game called El-quirkat, or Alquerque, as it is known today. The game is similar to checkers and may actually be the origin of checkers. The Moors of North Africa, who ruled much of Spain for more than seven centuries, until 1492, introduced the game into Europe. Several versions, played on square boards, are described in the *Book of Games*, written in 1283 under the direction of the Spanish king Alfonso the Wise. A diagram for this game was also found among those scratched in the roofing slabs of the temple for the Egyptian Pharaoh Seti I.

Awithlaknannai is played by the Zuni, a Pueblo (Native American) people of New Mexico. You may wonder how the game traveled so far from its original home. Probably the Spanish conquistadores brought it with them when they invaded the lands of the Pueblo starting in the sixteenth century, just as they brought the three-in-a-row game of Picaría (see page 10).

A game that is similar to Awithlaknannai, except for the shape of the board, is called Butterfly in Mozambique and Lau Kata Kati in India and Bangladesh. Here is another example of a game traveling far. We don't know whether it went from Africa to Asia or in the opposite direction.

Yoté, a game like checkers but more complicated, is popular in West Africa, especially in Senegal. Generally children scoop out holes in the ground and play with sticks or pebbles. This is a game that demands quick thinking, and a player who seems to be winning may suddenly find that he or she has actually lost the game.

Pong Hau K'i from Korea & China

TWO PLAYERS

Figure 14a

Pong Hau K'i (Pong-haw-kee) is a game from China. In Korea they call the game Ou-moul-ko-no, or Kono. As you can see, the board is very simple. Two people play on the five points where the lines intersect. Each player tries to block the other from moving.

MATERIALS

- **Sheet of construction paper**
- **Pen or marker**
- **Ruler**
- **2 counters for each player, of 2 different kinds (beans, buttons, or coins)**

DRAWING THE GAME BOARD

Draw two intersecting right triangles on the sheet of paper, as shown in the diagram. Make the board large enough so that there is lots of room to move the counters. **Figure 14a**

PLAYING THE GAME

The game begins with the counters placed on the board, as shown in the diagram. One player's counters are on the two lower points and the other player's counters are on the two upper points. **Figure 14b**

Player One moves one of his or her counters onto the center point. Then Player Two moves one of his or her counters onto the empty space. The players continue, with each player taking a turn to move a counter.

The game ends when one player wins by blocking the other player from moving. If the same set of moves is repeated three times, the game ends in a draw—no winner and no loser.

THINGS TO THINK ABOUT

Is it better to go first or second? How must you place your counters in order to block the other player?

Is it possible to play the game on this board with three counters for each player? How about one counter for each player? Explain.

Try to design a board that will allow each player to use three counters and at the same time follow the rules for Pong Hau K'i.

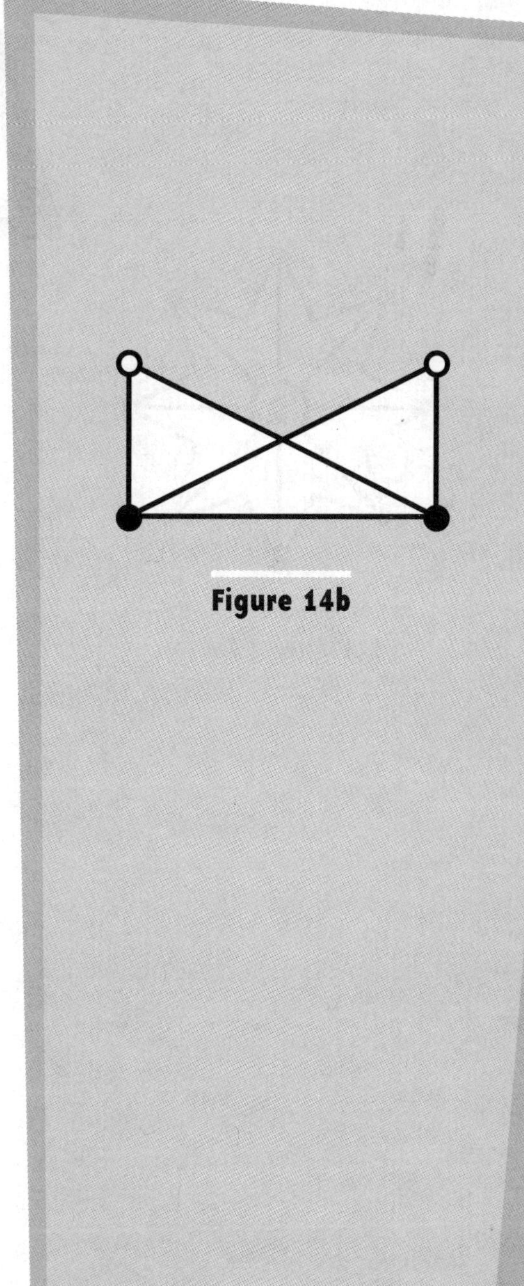

Figure 14b

Mu Torere from New Zealand

TWO PLAYERS

Figure 15a

Maori children in New Zealand have played Mu Torere (Moo Toh-RERE-uh) for as long as anyone can remember. The old people say that the Maori crossed the seas to New Zealand in seven canoes many centuries ago. They called the land Aotearoa in their language, which is related to the languages of Hawaii and Tahiti.

MATERIALS

- **Game board (see directions for Shisima on page 4)**
- **4 counters for each player, of two different kinds (call one set "white" and the other "black".)**

DRAWING THE GAME BOARD

The game board is an eight-pointed star with a space in the center called the *putahi*, or meeting place. The eight rays are called *kawai*, or branches. **Figure 15a**

Use the game board you created for Shisima (page 4), or follow the directions for making the octagonal Shisima board. Maori children draw the board on the ground with a pointed stick, or on a flat rock with a piece of charcoal.

PLAYING THE GAME

This is a blocking game; the goal is to block the other player from moving. To start, place the counters on the board. The four white counters occupy adjacent points of the star, and the four black counters occupy the four other points, as in the diagram. **Figure 15b**

Black starts, and players take turns moving their counters one at a time. A move can be made in one of three ways:

1. A counter can move from one point on the star (or octagon) to the next point, but only if the point is empty.

2. A counter can move from the *putahi* to an empty point.

3. A counter can move from the point to the *putahi*, but only if the opponent occupies the point(s) on one or both sides of that point. For example, Black can move into the *putahi* from point E or point H, but not from point F or point G.

The game ends when one player wins by blocking the other player from making any moves.

THINGS TO THINK ABOUT

What is the reason for rule number three above? See what happens when that rule is disobeyed.

Is it necessary for the winner to have one counter in the *putahi?* Why or why not?

What formation on the board leads to winning the game? (Hint: Some people call Mu Torere a "three-in-a-corner" game.)

CHANGING THE RULES

After each player has made two moves, any counter can be moved from a point to the *putahi.* How does this new rule change the moves leading to winning the game?

Try to play the game with three counters for each player. How must you move in order to win?

Try to play the game on a six-pointed star, with three counters for each player.

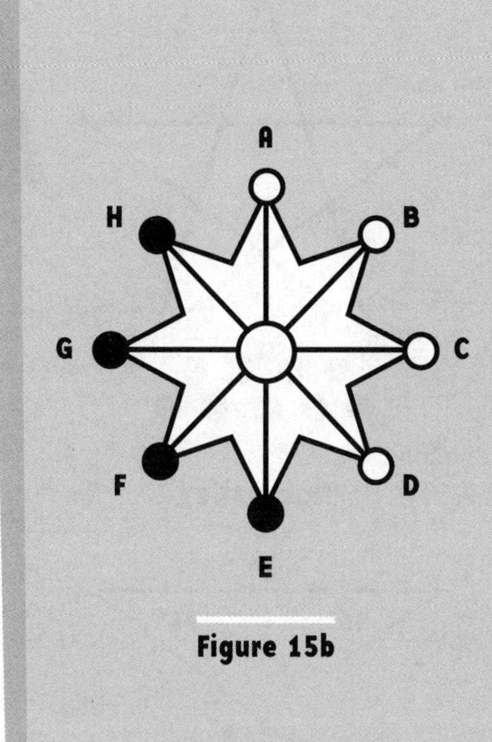

Figure 15b

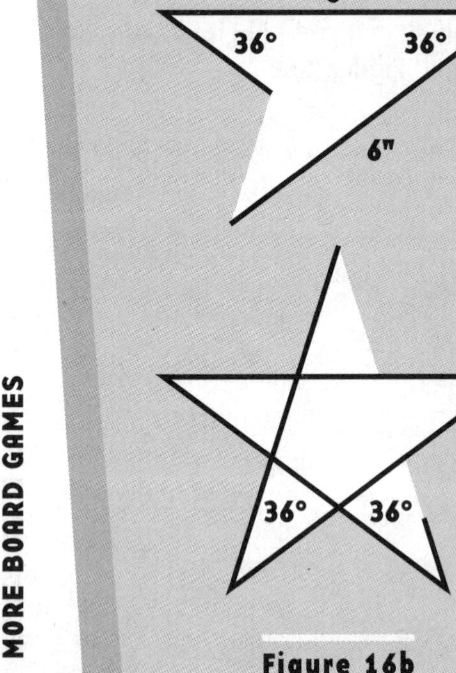

Figure 16a

Figure 16b

Pentalpha from Crete

ONE PLAYER

The name *pentalpha* comes from two Greek words. *Pent* means five, and *alpha* is the first letter of the Greek alphabet. The second letter is *beta*. Can you guess where we got the word *alphabet?* This game for one person is played on a five-pointed star called a pentagram. It is popular among people in Crete, an island in the Mediterranean Sea. **Figure 16a**

MATERIALS

- **Sheet of unlined paper**
- **Pencil, pen, or marker**
- **Ruler**
- **Protractor**
- **9 counters of any kind**

DRAWING THE GAME BOARD

Here are directions for drawing a really neat diagram. (Of course, you can draw one freehand that isn't so neat!)

1. Draw a horizontal line six inches (15cm) long above the center of the paper. Use the protractor to measure an angle of thirty-six degrees at each end of the line.
2. Draw six-inch lines to complete the two angles.
3. Measure an angle of thirty-six degrees at the end of each of these two lines.
4. Draw six-inch lines to complete the diagram. Mark the ten points where the lines intersect. **Figure 16b**

PLAYING THE GAME

This is a "placing" game. The counters are not moved after they have been placed on the board. Each counter is placed in three moves. It helps to count them out.

1. Place a counter on an empty point. Say "one."
2. Move it along a straight line so that it jumps over the next point (empty or not). Say "two." Remember the line must be straight.
3. Place it on the third point, which must be empty. Say "three."

Follow these rules for placing each counter until all nine counters are on the pentagram. Here is one move: **Figure 16c**

The goal is to place the nine counters on nine of the ten marked points of the board, one at a time, according to the rules above. It sounds easy but it is surprisingly tricky.

THINGS TO THINK ABOUT

Here is a hint: First place a counter on an inside point. Then fill in all four points on a line that lies as far as possible from that inside point. How would you complete the game? See Chapter 10 for a solution to this game.

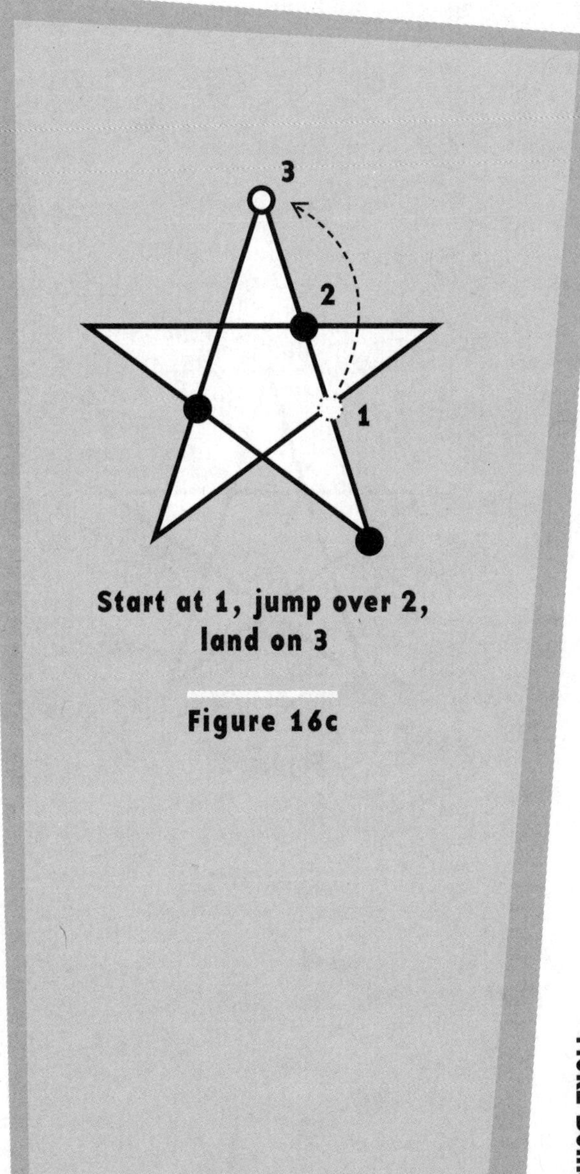

Start at 1, jump over 2, land on 3

Figure 16c

Kaooa from India

TWO PLAYERS

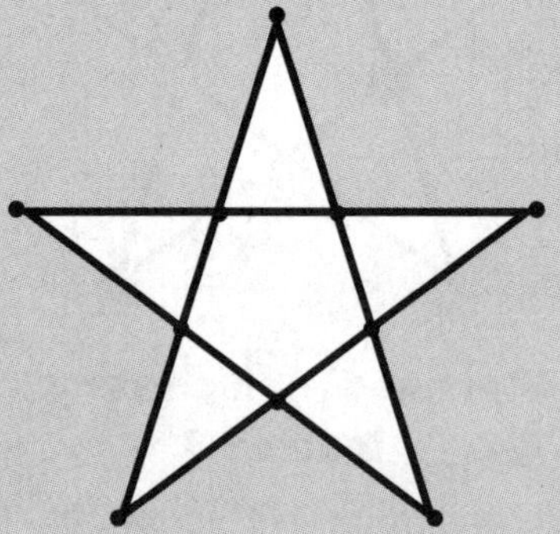

Figure 17

Children in India play Kaooa on a diagram in the form of a pentagram, or five-pointed star. Another name for the game is Vultures and Crows. The goal is for the vulture to capture the crows by jumping over them, or for the crows to corner the vulture so that the vulture can't move. **Figure 17**

MATERIALS

- **Game board (see the directions for Pentalpha on page 36)**
- **1 counter to represent the vulture (bean, button, or coin)**
- **7 counters to represent the crows (beans, buttons, or coins)**

PLAYING THE GAME

Player One places one crow on any point. Player Two places the vulture on an empty point.

Player One places the second crow on any empty point. Player Two moves the vulture one space along a line to an empty point.

They continue taking turns until all seven crows are on the board.

Then the players take turns moving one counter at a time to an adjacent empty point. Player One moves the crows and Player Two moves the vulture. The vulture may capture a crow by jumping over it along a line to an empty point. The vulture may make a series of captures on a single move.

The game ends when the vulture is trapped and can't move or when the vulture has captured at least four crows.

THINGS TO THINK ABOUT

Would the game work with fewer than seven crows? More than seven?

Awithlaknannai Native American

TWO PLAYERS

Almost one hundred years ago an anthropologist named Stewart Culin visited many parts of the world and wrote about the games that children and grown-ups played. He observed Zuni (Native American) children in New Mexico playing a game for two people in which they moved pebbles on a very long board scratched on a rock. Some children played a similar game on a shorter diagram. The game is called Awithlaknannai, referring to stones that were used to kill serpents.

MATERIALS

- **Sheet of construction paper or cardboard, at least 10 inches (25cm) long**
- **Ruler**
- **Pencil**
- **Pen or marker**
- **9 counters for each player, of 2 different kinds (stones, checkers, or coins)**

DRAWING THE GAME BOARD

Here is a diagram for a simple version of the game. You may want to make a longer board and use more than nine stones for each player. Stewart Culin claimed that he saw two people playing with twenty-three stones each on a board that was thirty-three inches long! The total number of counters is always one less than the total number of points on the board. **Figure 18**

Draw this diagram in pencil, then go over the pencil lines with a pen or marker. The diagram consists of two sets of triangles, one set of six triangles on each side of a long line. You might make a pattern of an isosceles triangle (two sides have the same length) and trace it twelve times to make a really neat diagram.

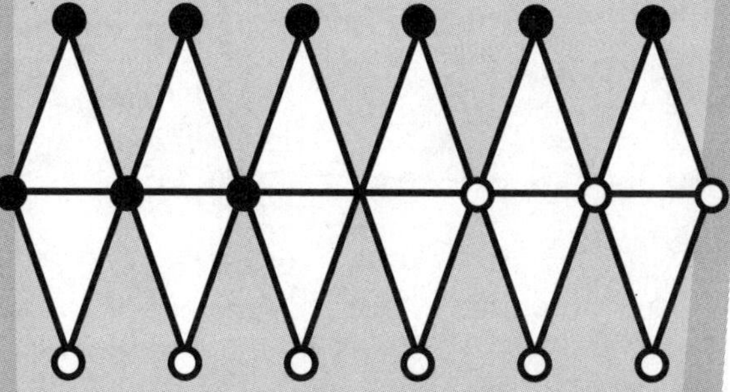

Figure 18

PLAYING THE GAME

Place the counters on the game board as shown in the diagram. Note that when the counters are in place, the center point, and only the center point, is empty, no matter how long a board you use.

Each player in turn moves one of his or her counters one space along a line to an adjacent empty point.

Or a player may jump over and capture an opponent's counter if the next space along a straight line is empty. A player may continue jumping with the same counter and capturing as long as possible.

A player who fails to jump loses the counter to the opponent. If a player has a choice of more than one jump, he or she may choose which jump to make.

The winner is the player who has captured all the opponent's counters, or as many as possible.

THINGS TO THINK ABOUT

Can you play with the same rules on a board that has an odd number like five, seven, or nine triangles on each side? Why or why not? Try it. Do you think Stewart Culin was correct when he wrote that each player in the game he watched had twenty-three stones? Where would the center point be on their game board?

CHANGING THE RULES

Play on a shorter board with fewer counters. Remember that only the center point is empty when you start. Then play on a longer board with more counters.

Butterfly from Mozambique

TWO PLAYERS

The game may be called Butterfly in Mozambique because of the shape of the board. Children in India and Bangladesh call the same game Lau Kata Kati.

MATERIALS

- **Sheet of unlined paper, at least 10 inches (25cm) long**
- **Ruler**
- **Pencil**
- **Pen or marker**
- **9 counters for each player, of 2 different kinds (beans, buttons, or coins)**

DRAWING THE GAME BOARD

Using your pencil and ruler, draw the board as shown in the diagram. Go over the lines with pen or marker. **Figure 19a**

PLAYING THE GAME

To start place the eighteen counters on the game board as shown in the diagram, leaving just the center point empty.

Each player in turn moves one of his or her counters one space along a line to an adjacent empty point.

Or a player may jump over and capture an opponent's counter if the next space along a straight line is empty. A player may continue jumping with the same counter and capturing as long as possible.

A player who fails to jump loses the counter to the opponent. If a player has a choice of more than one jump, he or she may choose which jump to make.

The winner is the player who has captured all the opponent's counters.

CHANGING THE RULES

Young children play on a smaller game board. Each player has six counters. **Figure 19b**

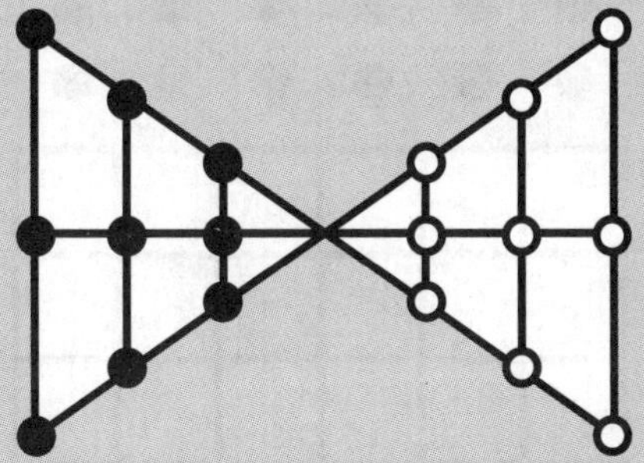

Figure 19a

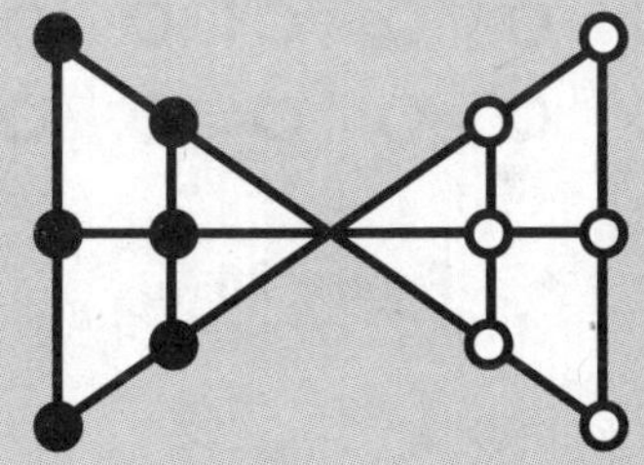

Figure 19b

Yoté from West Africa

TWO PLAYERS

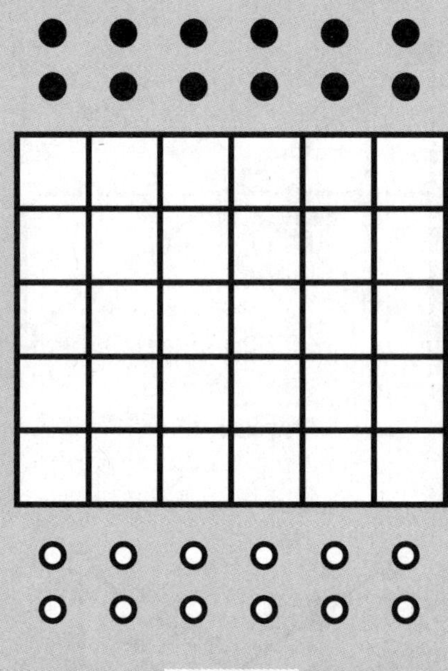
Figure 20

Yoté (YOH-tay) is similar to checkers. Children in West Africa scoop out holes in the sand, collect pebbles or bits of wood, and are ready to play the game. You may use checkers as counters and either make your own board or use part of a checkerboard.

MATERIALS

- **Scratch paper**
- **Pencil**
- **Ruler**
- **Piece of cardboard**
- **Marker**
- **12 checkers or other counters for each player, of 2 different kinds**

DRAWING THE GAME BOARD

This is the same game board that is used for playing Dara (page 18). It will have five rows of six spaces each.

1. Practice drawing your game board on scratch paper in pencil first. You need a rectangle divided into five rows of six squares each.
2. Then draw the game board on cardboard. First use a ruler to measure carefully, and mark the main points in pencil. Then draw the lines.
3. Go over the lines with a marker. **Figure 20**

PLAYING THE GAME

To Begin. Players take turns placing one counter at a time in any space on the board. They need not place all the counters before going on to the next stage. A player may keep some counters to be placed later.

To Move. Players take turns moving one counter at a time along a straight line to the next space, if it is empty. Moves are up or down or sideways, but not along a diagonal.

To Capture. A player may jump over an opponent's counter into the next space, if it is empty, and remove that counter from the board. In addition, this player may remove another of the opponent's counters from the board as a bonus.

To Finish. The winner is the player who has captured all of the opponent's counters. If each player has only three or fewer counters on the board, the game ends in a tie or a draw.

CHANGING THE RULES

Players must place all their counters on the board in the two rows closest to them before they move.

Play on a board with more or fewer squares. How many counters are needed for each type of board?

Penny	Nickel	Dime	Quarter	Total
head	head	head	head	4H
head	head	head	tail	3H, 1T

Table 1

4

Games of Chance

People have always hoped that they could find out what will happen in the future. A person might throw a penny and say: "If it comes up heads, I will do well on the math test tomorrow." Of course, doing well on the math test has nothing to do with the way a coin falls!

Games of chance arose from these attempts to foretell the future. People would throw dice or coins and look at the outcomes, the way the objects fell. Other objects used in such games were seashells, halves of nutshells, pits of certain fruits, tops, spinners, and marked sticks. People invented rules for winning and losing points.

How did people figure out these rules? They may have looked at how often a certain outcome will happen. For example, if you toss four coins many times, you are as likely to get four heads as four tails. That is because a coin is balanced—if it's a fair coin. Heads and tails are equally likely to occur. However, you are much more likely to get an outcome of two heads and two tails than either four heads or four tails.

Toss four different coins, like a penny, a nickel, a dime, and a quarter, about one hundred times and make a record of the outcomes. Or you can make a table with headings for the different coins. Figure out all the different ways that these four coins can fall. You should find sixteen ways.

Copy this table and finish it. How many of these ways are two heads and two tails? How many are four heads? How many are four tails? **Table 1**

What about a shell that is not well balanced? We cannot predict whether it is more likely to land with the opening up or the opening down. You might toss a shell many times and find that it lands with the opening up three times out of five. A different shell may have other outcomes.

When you play these games of chance, think about whether the games are fair. Do all the players have an equal chance of winning?

These games are often called "probability games." The study of probability is important in our life today. For example, probability is used in the insurance business and for predicting the weather.

Lu-lu from the Hawaiian Islands

TWO OR MORE PLAYERS

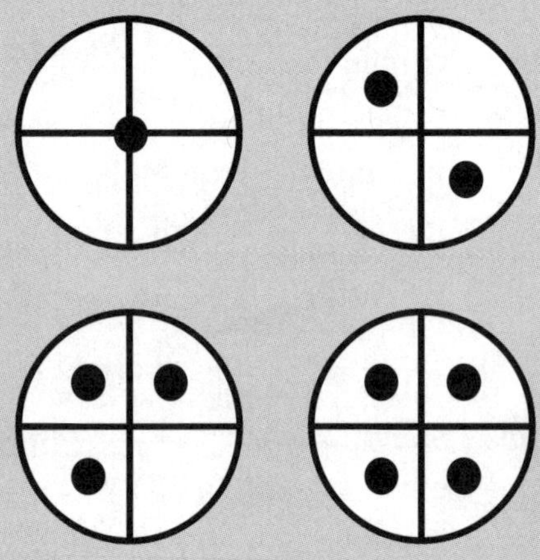

Figure 21

Lu-lu is a game played by the people who first came to the Hawaiian Islands. Stewart Culin, a famous anthropologist and collector of games, wrote about this game in an article published in 1899.

Polynesians sailed great distances across the Pacific Ocean from Asia to land on the Hawaiian Islands. The islands are of volcanic origin, and even today some volcanoes spew forth lava. Hawaiian children play Lu-lu with disks made of volcanic stone.

MATERIALS

- **4 disks, or circles cut from cardboard, about 1 inch (2.5cm) in diameter**
- **Marker or pen**
- **60 or more toothpicks or beans (or pencil and paper) to keep score.**

PREPARING THE DISKS

Mark one side of each disk with one, two, three, or four dots, as shown in the diagram. The marked sides are called the faces. **Figure 21**

PLAYING THE GAME

The players decide in advance how many rounds they will play. They take turns tossing the disks. Each player has two tosses before passing the disks to the next person. To toss the disks, a player holds the four disks in both hands and drops them onto the table or the ground.

If all the disks fall face up, the player scores ten points and tosses all four disks again. The number of dots that show on the second toss is added to the ten on the first toss to get the total score.

If one or more disks fall face down on the first toss, the player picks up only those face-down disks and tosses them again. The score is the total of all the dots on the four disks after the second toss. **Figure 22**

The winner is the player with the highest score at the end of the agreed-upon number of rounds. If they wish, the players can agree to play until one person reaches fifty points, or another agreed-upon number of points. To be fair, each person should have the same number of turns.

THINGS TO THINK ABOUT

Why do you suppose that a player scores ten points when all four disks fall face up? What is the highest score a player can have on one turn?

There are two different ways a player can score five points on the first toss. What are they? In how many ways can you score each of the other numbers, from zero to nine, on one toss of the disks?

CHANGING THE RULES

Let each player toss the disks just once on each turn. Which rules make for a better game, one toss or two tosses on each turn?

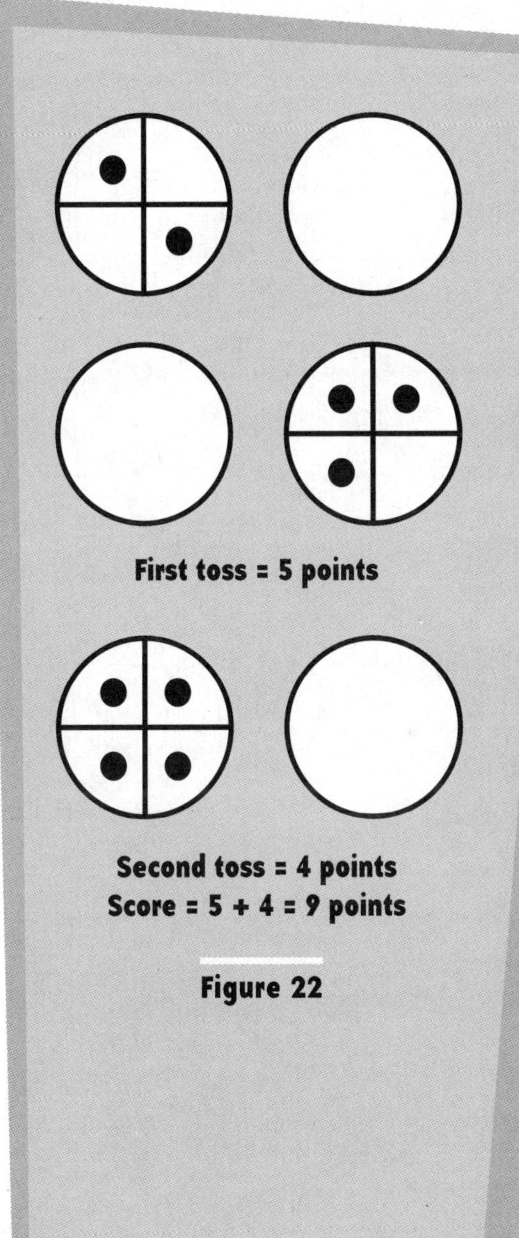

Figure 22

Native American Games

Native Americans have been playing games of chance for ages and ages. About one hundred years ago, Stewart Culin, an anthropologist, traveled around the continent to learn about these games. He collected them in a book, *Games of the North American Indians,* first published in 1907. He found that Native American children and grown-ups had many games that were similar to one another. The players would toss six or eight objects—sticks, peach pits, or walnut shells, for example. The sticks or fruit pits usually were plain on one side and colored or decorated on the other side. After each toss, the players counted how many of these objects fell with the decorated side up and how many had the plain side up. Players would earn points according to the way the objects fell. Their systems of scoring were often so complicated that the observer couldn't figure them out!

The Game of Dish and the Stick Game are simple forms of the games of the Native Americans. Children learned the simple forms to prepare for the complicated games played by grown-ups.

The Game of Dish Native American

TWO OR MORE PLAYERS

Some of the Native Americans who played this game, often called the Bowl Game, are the Seneca of New York, the Passamaquoddy of Maine, the Cherokee of Oklahoma, and the Yokut of California. The objects they used depended upon the things they found in their environment. The Seneca made buttons from the horns of elk. The Cherokee might have used beans. The Yokut used half shells of nuts filled with clay or pitch. Players tossed the playing pieces on flat baskets that the women had woven.

MATERIALS

- **4 playing pieces (bottle caps, peach pits, or walnut halves)**
- **Markers**
- **50 toothpicks or beans to keep score**
- **Wooden bowl, pie pan, or flat basket**

PREPARING THE PLAYING PIECES

Decorate each playing piece on one side with markers. Use a different pattern or color for each one. You might want to decorate the pieces with Native American patterns. Call the decorated side the "face" of the piece. **Figure 23**

PLAYING THE GAME

Players place the pile of toothpicks or beans in the center. Decide in advance how many rounds to play.

Players take turns tossing the playing pieces in the bowl. Hold the bowl with both hands and flip the pieces lightly in the air. Note whether they fall with the decorated sides (faces) up or down.

Players should be careful not to let pieces fall out of the bowl. They may decide to impose a penalty if that happens. Discuss this.

Figure 23

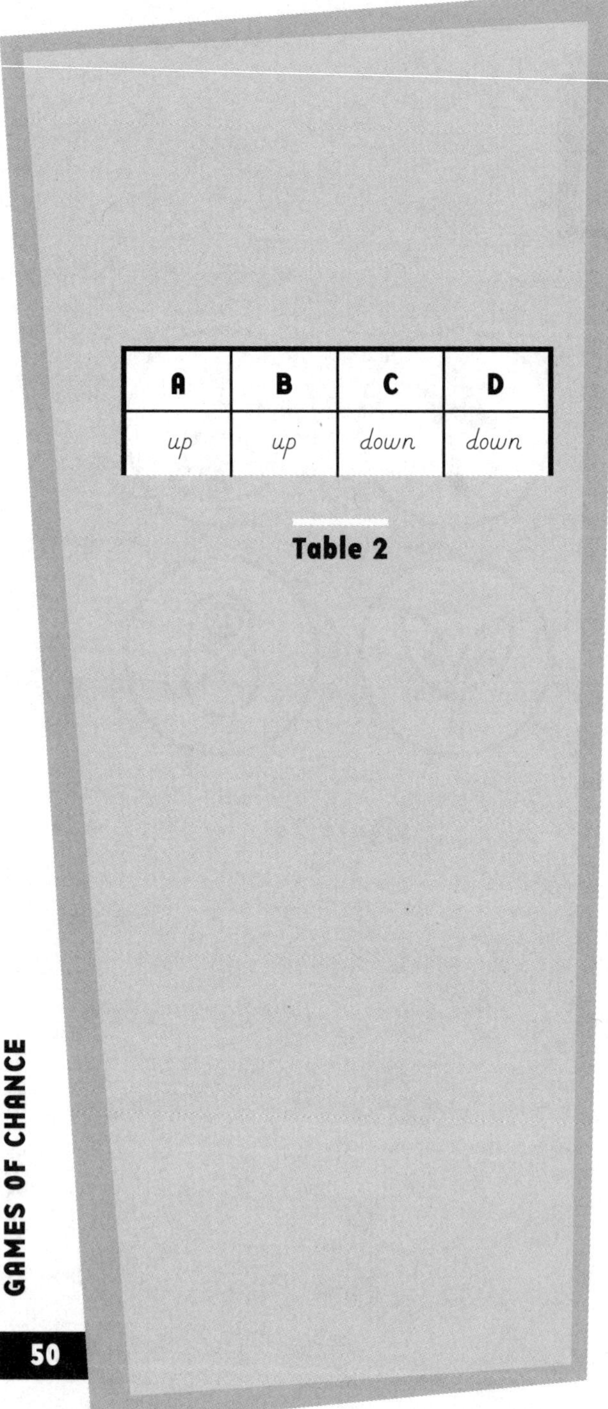

A	B	C	D
up	up	down	down

Table 2

SCORING

- All four up = five points
- Three up and one down = two points
- Two up and two down = one point
- One up and three down = two points
- All four down = five points

Count the number of points. Take that many toothpicks or beans from the pile and place them next to you. The player with the greatest number of toothpicks or beans at the end of the agreed-upon number of rounds is the winner.

THINGS TO THINK ABOUT

Is the scoring system fair? Note that an outcome of four up is scored the same as four down. Is this a fair way to score the game? One way to find out is to toss one playing piece twenty times. Keep track of the number of times it lands up and the number of times it lands down. Are they about the same, or is one outcome more likely than the other? Repeat the experiment. Is the scoring fair or unfair?

Can you find six different ways that the pieces can fall with two faces up and two faces down? Label the pieces A, B, C, and D, and make a list. Copy this table and finish it. **Table 2**

CHANGING THE RULES

Native Americans usually played these games with five, six, or more playing pieces. How would you score for five pieces? For six pieces?

Stick Game — Native American

TWO OR MORE PLAYERS

This Native American game is almost like the Game of Dish (page 49).

MATERIALS

- **4 popsicle sticks or tongue depressors**
- **Markers**
- **50 toothpicks or beans to keep score**

PREPARING THE PLAYING PIECES

Decorate each popsicle stick on one side with markers. Use a different pattern or color for each one. You might want to decorate the pieces with Native American patterns. Call the decorated side the "face" of the piece. **Figure 23**

PLAYING THE GAME

Players take turns. Each player holds the sticks in one hand and lets them fall to the ground or the table.

SCORING

- All four up = five points
- Three up and one down = two points
- Two up and two down = one point
- One up and three down = two points
- All four down = five points

Count the number of points. Take that many toothpicks or beans from the pile and place them next to you. The player with the greatest number of toothpicks or beans at the end of the agreed-upon number of rounds is the winner.

THINGS TO THINK ABOUT

Is this a fair way to score the game? Try to think of a better way to score. There are sixteen different ways that four sticks can fall. Here are three ways. How many more can you find? Copy this table and finish it. **Figure 24**

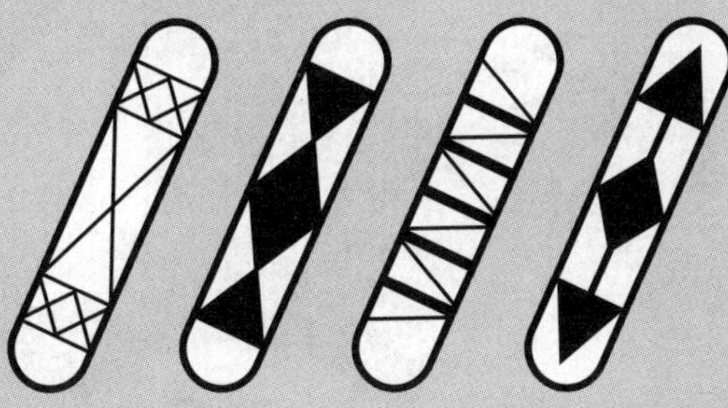

Figure 23

#1	#2	#3	#4
up	up	up	up
down	up	up	up
up	down	up	up

Figure 24

Igba-Ita from Nigeria

TWO OR MORE PLAYERS

Figure 25

Igba-Ita (EE-bah-EE-tah) is a game of chance played by the Igbo (EE-boh) people of Nigeria. The name means "pitch and toss." In the old days, groups of men, from two to twelve people, would gather in the marketplace for a game, while the women were busy buying and selling. The playing pieces were cowrie shells, which were used as coins in former times. Later they played the game with coins and called it Igba-Ego, which means "pitch the coins."

Early in the twentieth century an observer, G. T. Basden, wrote about the speed of the players: "I have watched players at this game, and it has always been quite beyond me to note the positions of the fall; the cowries have been counted and snatched up again long before I could begin to count."

Here is a simple version of the game.

MATERIALS

- **12 cowrie shells for each player (pasta shaped like shells are a good substitute)**

PLAYING THE GAME

To Begin. Decide in advance how many rounds to play. One person, called the challenger, picks up four shells. The other players agree that each will place one, two, or three shells into the center, called the "pot." The challenger tosses the four shells. The players count how many landed with the openings up and how many had the openings down. **Figure 25**

To Win the Pot. The challenger wins the pot when the shells land in any one of the following ways:

- All four with the openings up
- All four with the openings down
- Two up and two down

The challenger takes all the shells in the pot and continues to toss four shells.

To Continue. If the challenger loses, he or she puts the four shells into the pot. The next person becomes the challenger.

To Finish. The winner is the person who has the most shells. If at any point a player has too few shells to play, he or she drops out of the game.

THINGS TO THINK ABOUT

Is a shell just as likely to fall with the opening up as with the opening down? To find out, toss just one shell about thirty times. Keep a record of the outcomes. What is your conclusion? Repeat the experiment. Is the result the same or different?

Do the same with a coin. Is the result the same as with the shell?

Compare Igba-Ita with the Game of Dish (page 49). How are they the same? How are they different?

CHANGING THE RULES

Play the game by tossing three shells. What combinations will win so that it is a fair game?

Spin the Dreidel Jewish

TWO OR MORE PLAYERS

Figure 26a

During Hannukah, the Jewish Festival of Lights which usually occurs in December, children love to spin the dreidel (DRAY-del), a four-sided top. They celebrate the miracle that happened more than two thousand years ago in the year 165 B.C.E. (before the Common Era), when the brave Maccabees recaptured the temple of Jerusalem from the Syrians. Although there was hardly enough oil to keep the lamps burning just one night, somehow the oil lasted for eight days.

On each side of the dreidel is a Hebrew letter, spelling the initials of the message: *nes gadol hayah sham.* **Figure 26a**

In English the message is: "A great miracle happened there," and the letters are *G, M, H,* and *T.*

MATERIALS

- **Piece of cardboard, 3 inches (7.5cm) square**
- **Pencil, pen, or marker**
- **Thin dowel rod, lollipop stick, or short pencil**
- **Plasticine or molding clay**
- **Glue**
- **20 counters or coins for each player**

MAKING THE DREIDEL

1. Print one of the letters *G, M, H,* and *T* or the Hebrew letters nun, gimel, hay, and shin along each side of the square.
2. To locate the center of the cardboard square, draw the two diagonals of the square. Where the two lines intersect in the center, mark a dot.
3. Make a hole in the center and push the rod or stick through it.

4. Press plasticine or clay evenly around the stick where it meets the square underneath so the stick stays in place. You may want to use a little glue to hold the stick in place as well.
Figure 26b

PLAYING THE GAME

Decide in advance on the number of rounds to play. Players gather around the table. Each player puts two counters into the pot in the center.

The first player spins the dreidel and notes which letter is uppermost when the dreidel comes to rest. The player scores according to these rules (follow either the English or the Hebrew letters):

- G or *nun*—player wins nothing
- M or *gimel*—player takes the entire pot
- H or *hay*—player takes half the pot
- T or *shin*—player places a counter in the pot

Now, it is the next player's turn. Again, each player places two counters in the pot, and the game continues.

At the end, the player with the largest number of counters is the winner. If a player has no more counters before the game has ended, he or she is out of the game, unless the other players agree to let him or her continue.

THINGS TO THINK ABOUT

Should the dreidel fall more often on one side rather than another? Spin the dreidel twenty times and make a record of the outcomes. Suppose that one side of the dreidel is longer than the others. Or suppose that more clay has been put on one side than the others. How might that change the way a dreidel falls? Do you think that the rules for scoring are fair? Why or why not?

CHANGING THE RULES

Invent a different system of scoring. Play the game with your family or friends. Which system is more fair?

Figure 26b

Toma-Todo from Mexico

TWO OR MORE PLAYERS

Figure 27a

Children and grown-ups in Mexico like to play Toma-Todo. They spin a top in the shape of a hexagon, a six-sided figure. The name in Spanish is *pirinola,* or sometimes *topa,* which probably comes from the English word *top.* Try your luck with this game.

MATERIALS

- **Compass**
- **Pencil, pen, or marker**
- **Piece of cardboard, at least 4 inches (10cm) square**
- **Ruler**
- **Scissors**
- **Dowel rod, lollipop stick, or pencil stub**
- **Glue**
- **Plasticine or molding clay**
- **10 or more chips for each player, the same number of chips for each player**

MAKING THE TOP

1. Open your compass to a radius of two inches (5cm). Draw a circle on the cardboard.
2. Using a ruler, draw a diameter (a line through the center of the circle).
3. With the compass set at the same radius, place the compass point at one end of the diameter and make two arcs on the circle. Do the same at the other end of the diameter.
4. Connect the points to make a regular hexagon; all the sides have equal length and the angles have equal measure.
5. Draw the two other diameters. **Figure 27a**
6. Write the Spanish words (listed under Playing the Game) in each part of the hexagon.
7. Cut out the hexagon.
8. Make a hole in the center of the hexagon and push the rod or stick through it to serve as the spinning axis. Glue the stick to

the cardboard. Press a bit of plasticine or clay around the stick where it meets the hexagon underneath so that it stays in place. It also adds some mass to the spinner so that it spins better. **Figure 27b**

PLAYING THE GAME

Here is the translation of the Spanish instructions:

SIDE	SPANISH	ENGLISH
1	Toma uno	Take one
2	Toma dos	Take two
3	Toma todo	Take all
4	Pon uno	Put one
5	Pon dos	Put two
6	Todos ponen	All put

Players sit in a circle around the table or on the floor, each with a pile of counters or chips. They decide in advance on the number of rounds to play. Each player places two chips in the pot in the center. The first player spins the pirinola once and notes the side that is uppermost when the top comes to rest. The Spanish words on that side tell what to do. The player may be told to take one or two chips or all the chips from the pot. Or the player may be told to place one or two chips into the pot. "Todos ponen" means that every player must place two chips into the pot.

The next player in the circle spins the top. Play continues in this way. If at the end of a turn the pot has fewer than three chips, each player adds two or more chips to the center.

If a player doesn't have enough chips to play, he or she drops out of the game.

The player who has the most chips at the end is the winner.

THINGS TO THINK ABOUT

Compare the shape of the pirinola with that of the dreidel (page 54). Compare the rules for the two games. How does the shape of the spinner affect the rules of the game?

CHANGING THE RULES

Invent a game with a spinner in the shape of a regular octagon. To construct an octagon, see the instructions for Shisima (page 4). What rules would you invent for the game?

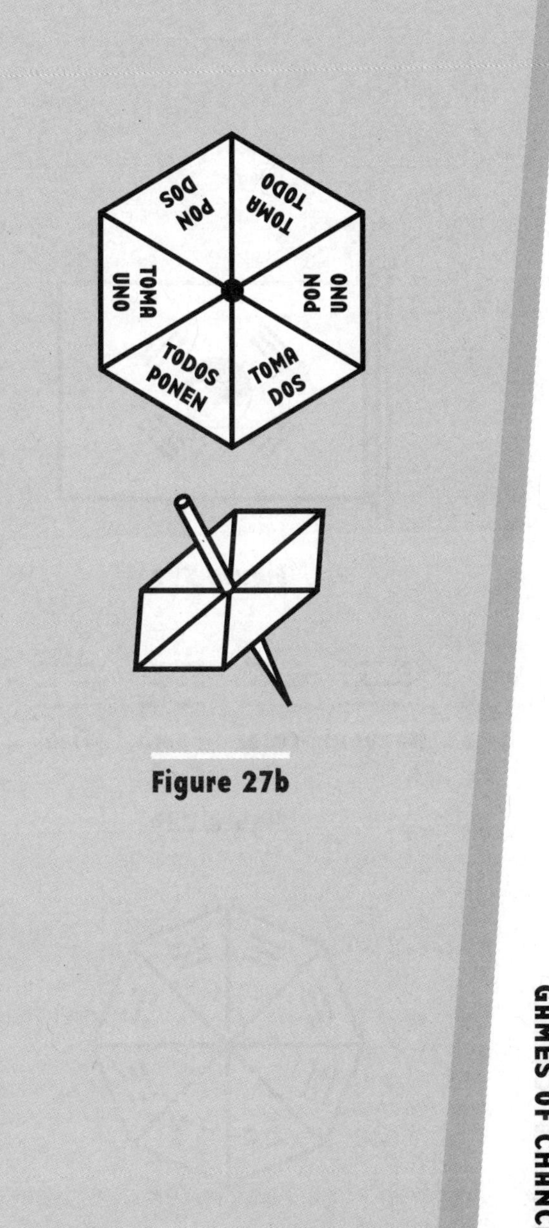

Figure 27b

Trigrams & Good Luck from East Asia

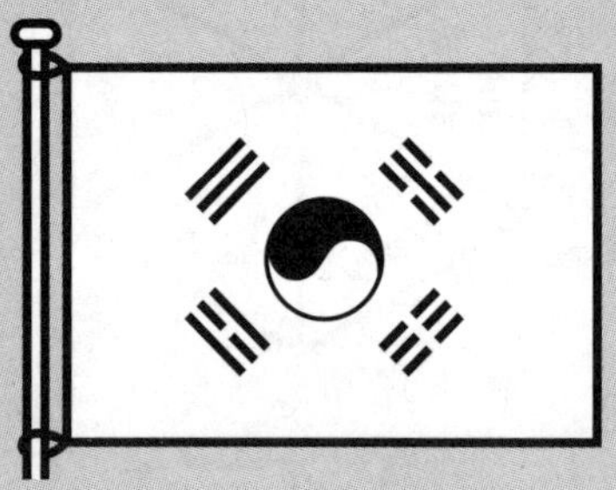

Figure 28a

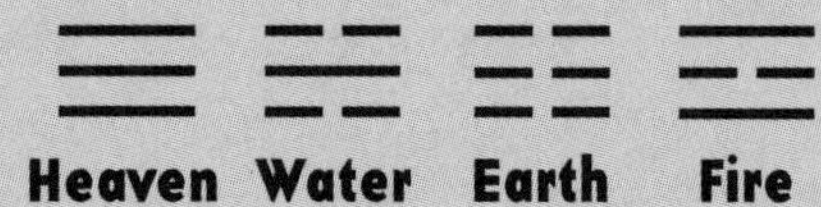

Figure 28b

Figure 28c

Here is a picture of the flag of South Korea. **Figure 28a**

In the center of the flag is the yin-yang symbol. Around it are four signs. Each sign consists of three lines, either solid lines or broken lines. These signs are called trigrams. What does *tri* mean? (Think of words like triangle and tricycle.) Each sign has a meaning. **Figure 28b**

These signs were invented in China several thousand years ago. The Korean and Japanese people later adopted them. Some people thought that they brought good luck. The Koreans liked them so well that they put them on their flag.

THINGS TO DO

There are eight different trigrams. Draw the four missing signs. What things in nature do you want them to stand for?

Make a game with the eight trigrams. Here is one way. Make an eight-sided top or spinner in the shape of a regular octagon. See Shisima (page 4) for instructions on drawing the octagon. **Figure 28c**

Read the rules for Toma-Todo (page 56) to help you make up the rules for your game.

THINGS TO THINK ABOUT

Trigrams are like writing. People could read three solid lines as "sky" or "heaven." What sign is opposite "heaven" on the flag? Compare the two sets of lines. Now look at the sign for "fire." What is the opposite of "fire" on the flag? Compare the arrangement of lines in these two trigrams.

The Hexagrams of I Ching from China

For more than two thousand years the Chinese have used the book called *I Ching*, or *Book of Changes*, to try to foretell the future. *I Ching* lists sixty-four different hexagrams, or sets of six solid or broken lines. A hexagram consists of two trigrams (see page 58). Here are some examples: **Figure 29**

A person throws six sticks to find out his or her special hexagram. Each hexagram has some wise advice to go with it. A person has to figure out how these words of wisdom apply to his or her problem. People use the hexagrams to help them solve their own problems.

THINGS TO THINK ABOUT AND DO
How many more hexagrams can you draw? Try to draw all sixty-four hexagrams. Work out a system so that you don't miss any. Why do you think these figures are called hexagrams? Do you know other words that start with "hexa"?

Figure 29

5

Puzzles with Numbers

Some of the puzzles in this section are very old. The stories in them may have been told by merchants traveling with their goods through Asian countries—India, China, the Arab lands. In all these countries there was great interest in mathematics. Muslim traders brought these puzzles to Africa.

People who posed these puzzles dressed them up to suit their own customs. A story about camels in one country might become a problem about horses or sheep in another place. A puzzle with letters of the alphabet used the letters that people knew (you will use the Latin letters of the English alphabet). Magic squares had different meanings in various cultures and even used different numerals.

In this book several puzzles were brought up to date. In two puzzles we see that doubling the number of grains of rice over and over again is like counting your ancestors. The last two puzzles compare the postal codes we use today with the markings that Africans made on bone about twenty-five thousand years ago!

Secret Code Part I Ancient Hebrew & Greek

Roy and Barbara use a secret code to figure out the value of their names. Roy's name has a value of fifty-eight. Barbara's name has a value of forty-three. Roy's name has only three letters, while Barbara's has seven letters. Although Barbara's name is much longer than Roy's, the value is smaller. Does that surprise you?

Roy and Barbara are using a system that is very old. It goes back more than two thousand years to the ancient Hebrews and Greeks. Instead of inventing symbols for numbers, as the ancient Egyptians had done, the Hebrews and Greeks used the letters of their alphabets as numerals. The symbols that we use today, like 0, 1, 2, and 3, were invented in India and brought to Europe much later by Arabic-speaking North Africans. We call them Indo-Arabic (or Hindu-Arabic) numerals.

The first two letters of the Hebrew alphabet are *aleph* and *bet*. In the Greek alphabet the first two letters are *alpha* and *beta*. You can guess where the English word alphabet comes from! The Hebrews and Greeks used those letters to stand for the numbers 1 and 2.

MATERIALS

- **Sheet of paper**
- **Pen or pencil**

DOING THE PUZZLE

We will use the English alphabet. Copy the alphabet on a sheet of paper and write the value of each letter under it. Use all the numbers from one to twenty-six. **Figure 30a**

Roy figured out the value of his name this way:
R=18, O=15, Y=25. 18+15+25=58.

Barbara's name adds up like this: 2+1+18+2+1+18+1=43.

A	B	C	D	E	F	G	H	I	J	K	L	M
1	2	3	4	5	6	_	_	_	10	_	_	_

N	O	P	Q	R	S	T	U	V	W	X	Y	Z
_	15	_	_	_	_	20	_	_	_	_	_	26

Figure 30a

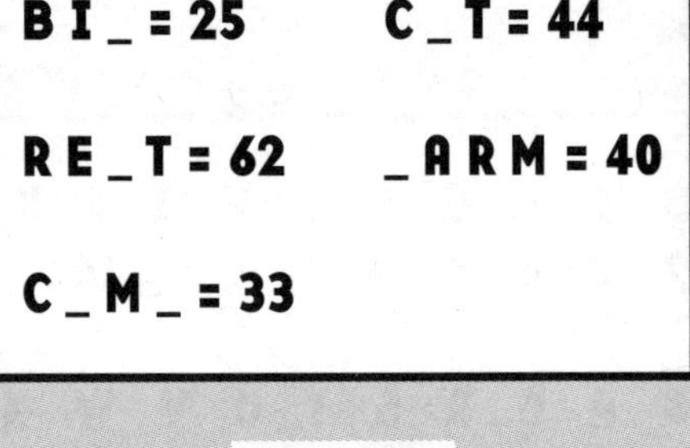

Figure 30b

THINGS TO DO

Here are some ideas for having fun with numbers:

What is the value of your name? Figure out the values of the names of your friends and family members. Do longer names always have higher values?

Here are words with one or two letters missing. The value of the whole word is given. Copy them and fill in the missing letters. **Figure 30b**

Here is a game you can play with your friends. Each person writes five words and figures out the value of each word. Then rewrite the words and their values on another sheet of paper, but leave out one or two letters. Exchange papers and fill in the missing letters. Then check the answers.

How many words can you find that add up to thirty? To forty-five? Select a number and find as many words as possible having that value.

Secret Code Part II Ancient Hebrew & Greek

Using letters as numbers can be clumsy. How would you write a number like 278?

The Hebrews and Greeks solved that problem for numbers that went into the hundreds. This is how they would have done it using the English alphabet. We'll call this the Letter-Numeral system. **Figure 31a**

In this system, ME=40+5=45

BOY=2+60+700=762

For larger numbers, they placed bars or accents on the letters.

DOING THE PUZZLE

These words are actually Letter-Numerals. What is each number? **Figure 31b**

THINGS TO THINK ABOUT

Can you use the Letter-Numeral system to spell more English words? Why are there so few words?

Invent a way to show numbers like 1,000, 2,000, 30,000, and other large numbers.

A	B	C	D	E	F	G	H	I
1	2	3	4	5	6	_	_	_
J	**K**	**L**	**M**	**N**	**O**	**P**	**Q**	**R**
10	20	_	_	_	_	_	80	90
S	**T**	**U**	**V**	**W**	**X**	**Y**	**Z**	
100	200	_	_	_	_	700	800	

Figure 31a

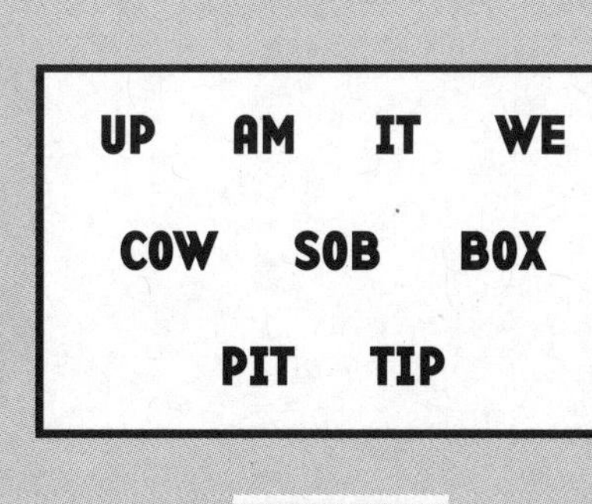

Figure 31b

Magic Squares Part I from West Africa

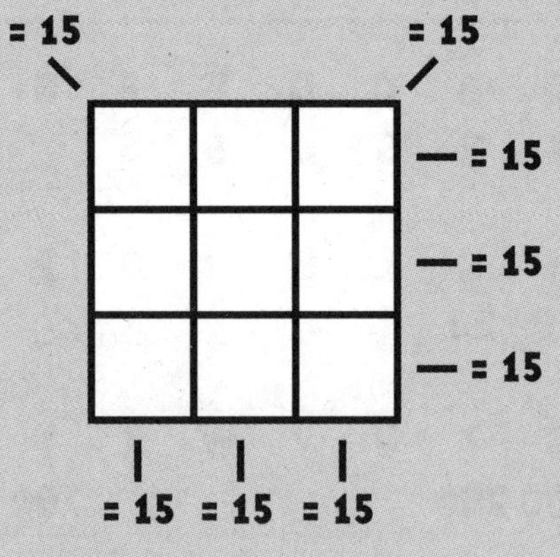

Figure 32a

Ahmed popped a peanut into his mouth just as his friend Daoud came into view.

"Let's play Antelope and Leopard," called Daoud. "Here, I have three times fifteen stones."

Ahmed scooped out the earth to make the nine holes in the ground while Daoud emptied his pockets. Although Ahmed had never played the game himself, he had watched many times as the older boys challenged one another to construct the magic square.

The goal was to place the forty-five stones in the square of nine holes so that the sum of the numbers of stones was fifteen in each row, each column, and the two main diagonals. Each hole must contain a different number of stones, and each of the numbers from one to nine must be used just once. **Figure 32a**

"You be the antelope; I'll be the leopard," said Daoud. "If you can't make the magic square, I will eat you! What will you put up—something good to eat?"

Ahmed held out a handful of his precious peanuts. Daoud's eyes lit up, and he smacked his lips. Ahmed laid the peanuts carefully on the ground, next to the three-by-three array of holes.

Ahmed picked up fifteen of the stones. He remembered that the middle number was always five. That left ten stones to be divided between two holes on either side of the middle square. But which two holes? How should he split up the remaining ten stones? Hadn't he seen the older boys place one stone below the five, and nine above the five? It was worth trying. He glanced at his friend's face as he placed his stones in the holes. Daoud did seem rather disappointed. Was he worried that he might not win the peanuts? **Figure 32b**

Ahmed decided to concentrate on the bottom row as his next move. He already had one stone in the middle square, so he would need fourteen more stones for the other two spaces. Seven and seven would not be right, because each number must be used only once. He picked up the fourteen stones and divided them into two piles of nine and five. No, that can't be right. He had already used five in the center and nine above it.

Just then the skies opened up and sheets of rain began to fall. Ahmed scooped up his peanuts, and both boys ran for shelter. In a moment their magic square was washed away without a trace. Well, they could always make another one.

THINGS TO DO

Can you finish the magic square?

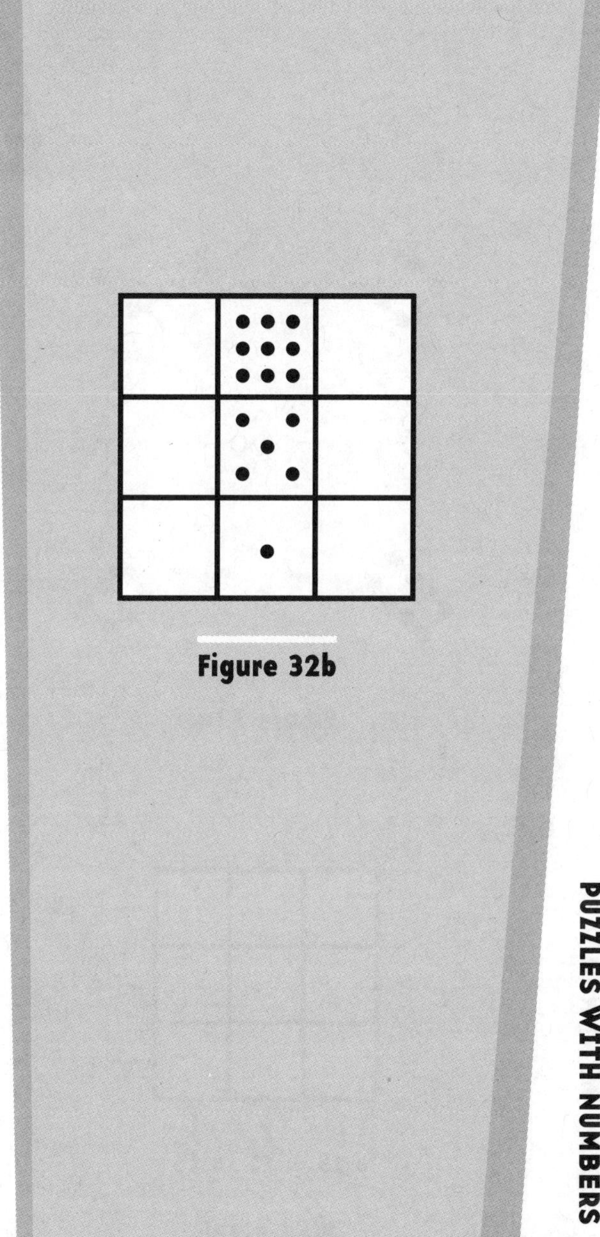

Figure 32b

Magic Squares Part II from China

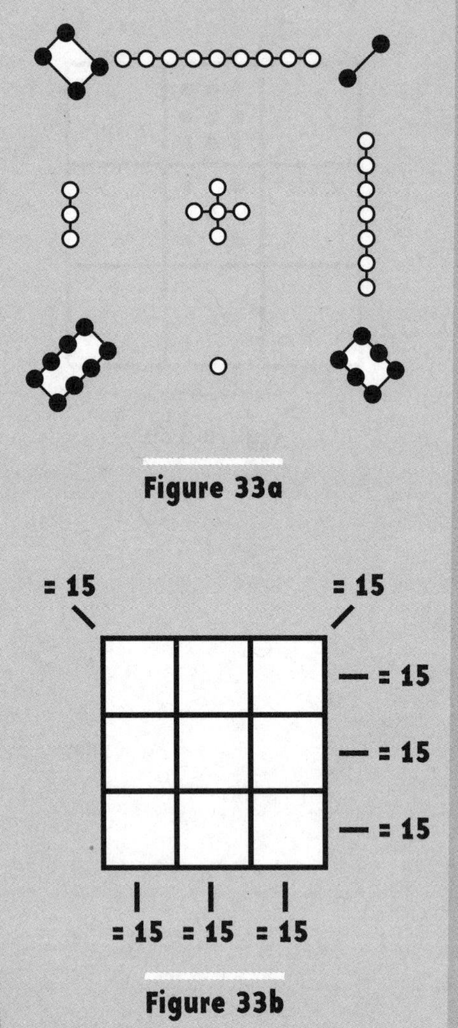

Figure 33a

Figure 33b

According to Chinese legend, this happened more than four thousand years ago. The emperor was sailing down the River Lo with his court. Suddenly a turtle appeared. On its back was a pattern of dots. Each part of the pattern had a different number of dots. **Figure 33a**

MATERIALS

- **Sheet of paper**
- **Pen or pencil**

DOING THE PUZZLE

Draw a three-by-three square as shown here: **Figure 33b**. Count the number of dots in each part of the pattern in figure 33a. Place those numbers in the cells of the square. What number belongs in the middle? What numbers are in the corners?

The Chinese thought this square was magical. To find out why, add the three numbers in each row, each column, and each diagonal—eight different sums.

The sum is always the same number: fifteen. This is called the "magic sum" of the "magic square." The ancient Chinese and other peoples thought they could tell fortunes by using magic squares.

THINGS TO FIGURE OUT

Copy the squares shown here: **Figure 33c**. Complete each square so that the magic sum is fifteen. Use each of the numbers from one to nine exactly once. Check all eight sums in each square.

What number is in the center? What numbers are in the corners? What numbers are in the two diagonals?

Copy the squares shown here: **Figure 33d**. Complete each square so that the magic sum is eighteen. Use each of the numbers from two to ten exactly once. Check all eight sums in each square.

What number is in the center? What kind of numbers are in the corners? What numbers are in the two diagonals?

Make two copies of each square. Use each of the numbers from zero to eight exactly once. Complete each square in two different ways. **Figure 33e**

What is the magic sum? What number is in the middle?

Make a three-by-three magic square using the even numbers from two to eighteen exactly once. What number should go in the middle? What do you think will be the magic sum?

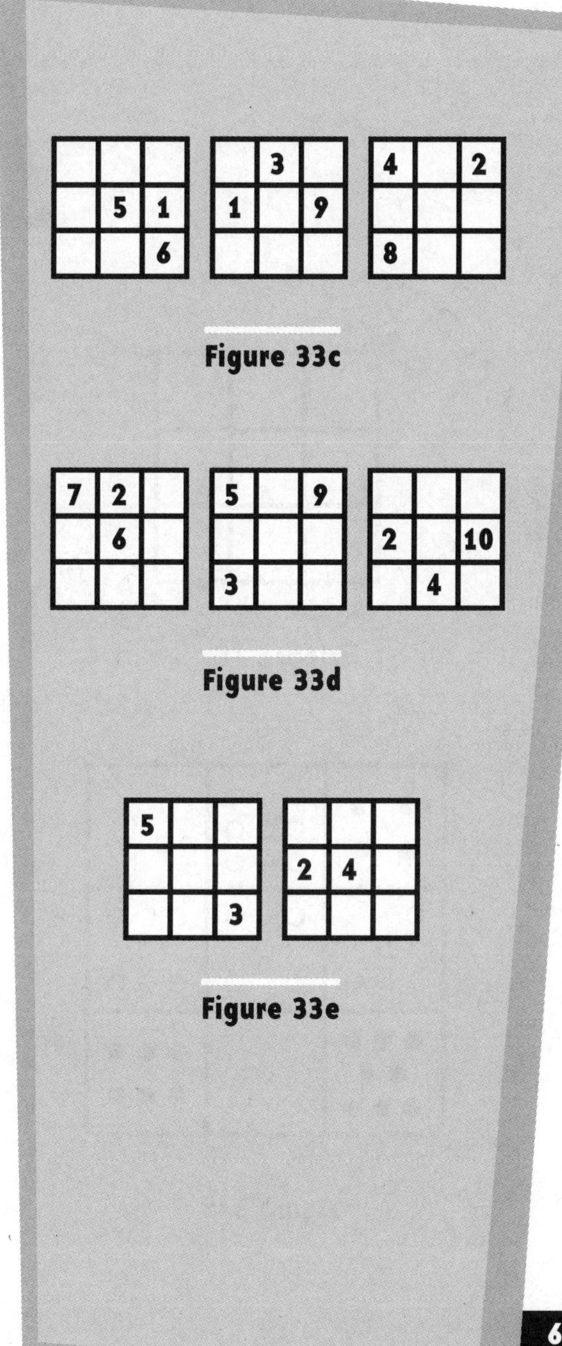

Figure 33c

Figure 33d

Figure 33e

Magic Squares Part III

Figure 34a

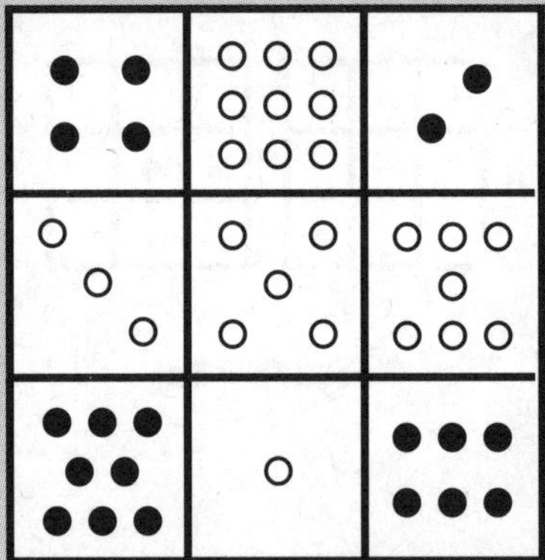

Figure 34b

There are eight different three-by-three magic squares using the numbers from one to nine exactly once each (see Magic Squares, Part I, page 64). You can make all eight magic squares by drawing just one square in a special way.

MATERIALS

- 2 sheets of plain paper
- Pen or pencil
- 2 colored markers (black and red, or two other colors)
- Sheet of scrap paper
- Ruler

DRAWING THE MAGIC SQUARE

1. Draw a large square. Divide it into nine small squares. Go over the lines with a black or dark-colored marker. **Figure 34a**
2. With the markers copy the pattern of dots below. Make the even numbers black and the odd numbers red (or two other different colors). Place scrap paper under the sheet of paper, because the marks will probably go through the paper. **Figure 34b** How many dots are in the whole magic square?

This pattern is similar to the markings the Chinese emperor saw on the turtle in the River Lo more than four thousand years ago, according to a Chinese myth (see Magic Squares, Part II, page 66).

Turn the paper over. If the lines and dots don't show through clearly, go over them with markers. Now you have another magic square on the back of the sheet.

THINGS TO DO

Turn or flip your magic square so that the dots match the numbers in the magic squares shown here:
Figure 34c

Use your dot-numeral magic square to find the other five magic squares. Draw them on a separate sheet of paper, using numerals instead of dots.

THINGS TO FIGURE OUT

For each magic square, state the number in the center. What is the magic sum of each square? What is the sum of all the numbers in the magic square? Explain how all these numbers are connected.

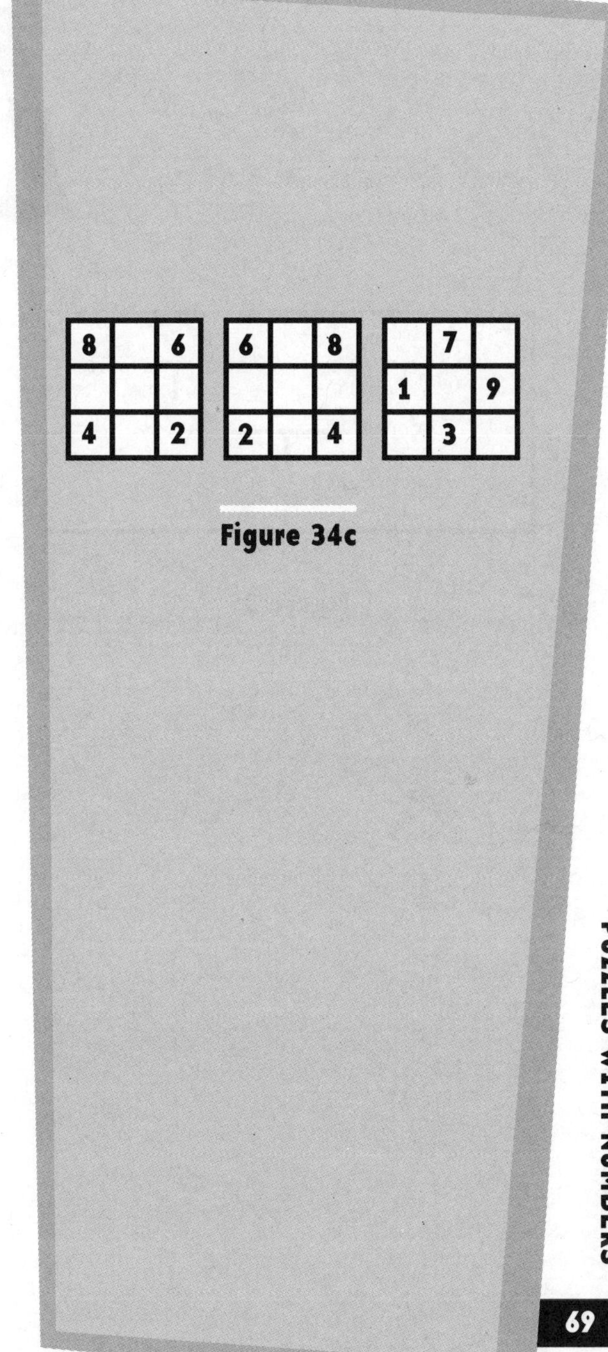

Figure 34c

Counting Your Ancestors

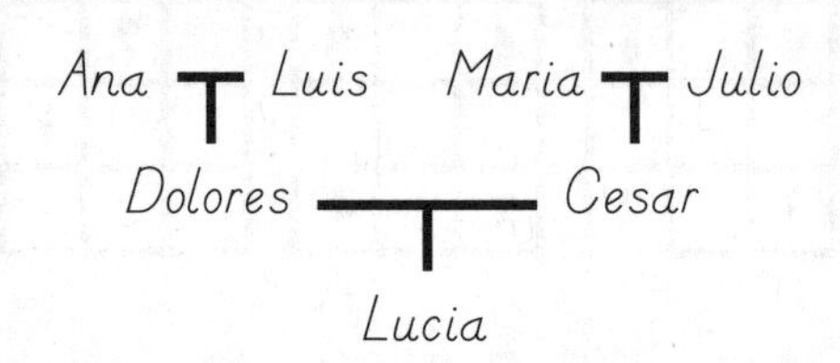

Figure 35

In most cultures, people have a great deal of respect for their ancestors and other older people. Ancestors are your father and mother, your grandparents, and their parents and grandparents going all the way back in time.

Lucia's parents and grandparents came to the United States from Mexico about twenty years ago. She made a "family tree" that looked like this: **Figure 35**

Dolores and Cesar are Lucia's parents. Dolores's parents are Ana and Luis. Cesar's parents are Maria and Julio. Lucia thinks of her parents as being one generation back in time from her generation. Her grandparents are two generations back from Lucia's. In three generations, including herself, Lucia counts seven people.

How many great-grandparents does Lucia have? How many people are in Lucia's family tree in four generations, counting herself?

Lucia wondered how many ancestors she had going back ten generations. That would take her family back to about the year 1730, when some of her ancestors traveled to Mexico from Spain. She made a table to organize her calculations. **Table 3**

MATERIALS

- **Sheet of paper**
- **Pen or pencil**
- **Ruler**

DOING THE PUZZLE

Copy the table and help Lucia to complete it for ten generations. She decided that she had 1,022 ancestors (not counting herself). Is this correct?

THINGS TO THINK ABOUT

How far back in time can you continue the table? Study the numbers in each column. What patterns can you find? Is there a way to figure out how many ancestors you have going back twenty generations without having to make a table?

Number of generations	Number of ancestors in this generation	Total
1	1	1
2	2	3
3	4	7
4	8	15
5		

Table 3

Rice Multiplies from Asia

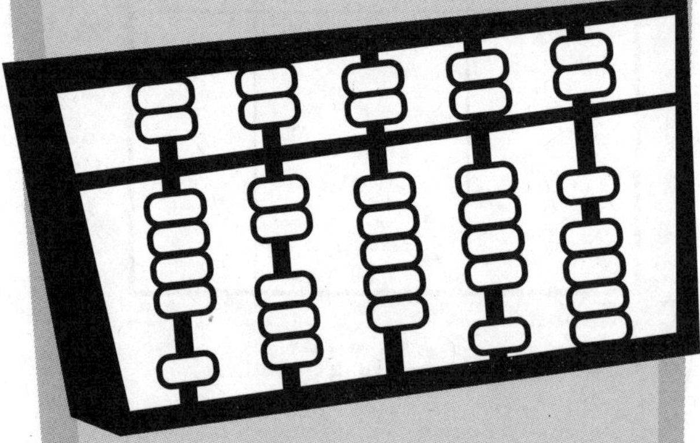

There is an old tale told in China, India, Persia (now called Iran), and other Asian countries. The story is about a wise old man who showed the king the solution to a problem that no one in the king's court could solve.

"Ask for anything you desire," the king said to the wise man in gratitude.

The wise man thought for a while. Then he said to the king, "Your majesty, I do not need much. Just give me one grain of rice today, two grains of rice tomorrow, and four grains of rice the day after tomorrow. Each day give me twice as many grains as the day before until the end of the month."

The king was surprised that the wise man asked for so little, but he ordered the treasurer of the kingdom to carry out the request.

THINGS TO FIGURE OUT

Figure out how many grains of rice the wise man received on the eleventh day. How many grains of rice should the wise man receive on the twenty-first day? Can you make a good estimate without doing a lot of arithmetic? On the thirty-first day the wise man should receive well over a billion grains of rice. Figure out the exact number. You can check your answer in Chapter 10.

THINGS TO THINK ABOUT

Could the treasurer count out so many grains? Were farmers able to grow that much rice?

Dividing the Camels from North Africa

A merchant was riding home on his camel after selling all his goods at the town market. He stopped at an inn for the night. Just as he was ready to go to sleep after his tiring day, he heard loud voices below his window. He went out to see what was going on and found three men with a large herd of camels.

"What can I do with half a camel?" shouted the oldest man.

"How can we split a camel into little pieces?" complained another.

As the argument went on and on, the merchant wondered whether he would get any sleep. He decided to try to settle the matter.

"Pardon me, good fellows," he said as sweetly as he could. "Perhaps I can help you solve your problem."

The three men started shouting all at once. The merchant did his best to calm them down, and at last he learned what the argument was about.

The three men were brothers. Their father had died, leaving them his thirty-five camels. According to his will, the oldest brother was to have half the herd. The middle brother would receive one-third of the camels, while the youngest would get one-ninth. No matter how they figured it out, using the instructions in the will, they always had to cut camels into pieces.

"Ah, now I see how I can help you," said the merchant, a man with a great deal of experience with numbers. "I will add my fine camel to your thirty-five camels. Then you will see how neatly you will be able to divide the herd, without having to cut up your animals."

The brothers were happy to have such wise advice. They smiled as the merchant divided the thirty-six camels among them, because each would receive more than he expected. To the oldest went half the herd—eighteen camels. The middle brother got one-third, or twelve camels. The youngest received four camels, one-ninth of the herd. Altogether, the brothers received thirty-four animals, and two camels were left over.

"You must grant that I made a fair division," said the merchant. "Now I will take back the animal I lent you. And I will take the other camel as my reward for dividing the herd among you to everyone's satisfaction."

THINGS TO FIGURE OUT

How many camels would each brother have received if they had divided thirty-five camels according to their father's will? Explain how the clever merchant could divide the herd so that all the camels remained whole and two were left over. What was wrong with the instructions in the father's will?

The Ishango Bone from Congo

An archaeologist digging in the vicinity of a village called Ishango, in the eastern part of Congo, found an unusual bone. A bit of quartz was attached at one end, and the bone was covered with notches. Who were the people that made these marks? When did they live? What do the marks mean?

Here are sketches of two sides of the Ishango bone. Next to each sketch is a set of numbers telling how many notches appear. Study the numbers and decide how they are related to one another. **Figure 36**

Dr. Jean de Heinzelin, the Belgian scientist who discovered the bone in the 1950s, thought that it was about nine thousand years old. Counting the groups of notches, he decided that they showed doubling—3 and 6, 4 and 8—and prime numbers—11, 13, 17, 19. A prime number is divisible only by itself and one. Another scientist, Alexander Marshack, examined the bone under a microscope and decided that the notches marked the days of a six-month lunar calendar, a calendar based on cycles of the moon.

In the 1980s Dr. de Heinzelin and a team of scientists went back to Ishango to dig further. With new methods of dating such materials, they came to a surprising conclusion. The bone was twenty thousand to twenty-five thousand years old!

THINGS TO THINK ABOUT

What evidence do you see for doubling numbers? Do you find prime numbers? What evidence do you see for a calendar based on the cycles of the moon? The period of one cycle is about 29½ days. Can you combine groups of notches to make sums of twenty-nine or thirty?

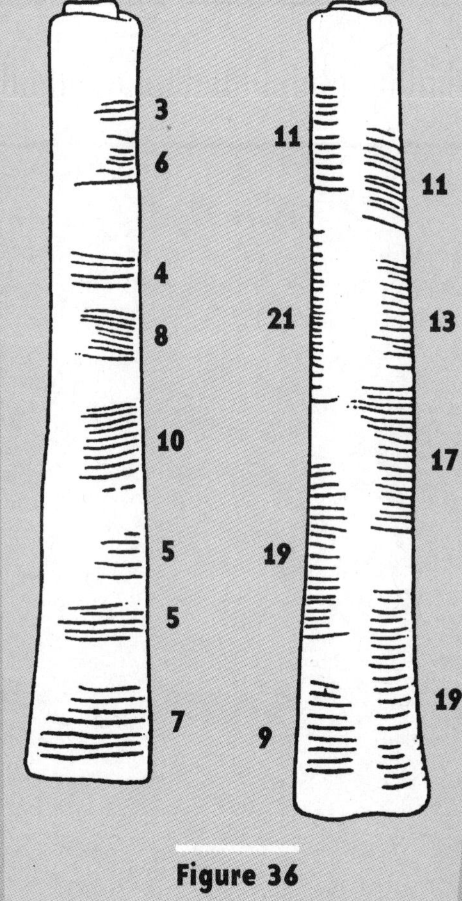

Figure 36

Postal Codes from the U.S.A.

Figure 37a

Usually printed on the bottom edge of letters and magazines, we see rows of long and short lines. We saw similar-looking lines—notches made more than twenty thousand years ago (see page 75)—on the Ishango bone. What do they mean?

Let's look at the codes the United States Post Office uses. Machines invented by smart scientists can read these codes and sort the mail. Imagine how much time and energy that saves!

I have a return envelope sent by the Children's Defense Fund in Baltimore, Maryland 21298-9642. This combination of long and short marks is the code for the nine digits in the address. **Figure 37a**

Years ago, when the post office started to use postal zip codes, five digits were enough. Later they added four more digits to specify individual buildings and groups of buildings and shorten the time it took to process the mail. Here are some five-digit zip codes. **Figure 37b**

THINGS TO THINK ABOUT AND DO

Examine the five-digit codes. How many marks are needed for each number from zero to nine? How many are short and how many are long?

Make a list of all the numbers from zero to nine. Write the correct code next to each number. Are all the codes different from one another?

Write all the different ways you can arrange three short marks and two long marks. How many ways have you found?

Look at the nine-digit zip code of the Children's Defense Fund. Here are some instructions for reading the code. Ignore the first bar and the last bar. You now have fifty marks for ten digits. The tenth digit is a checking number. You may ignore it. Can you read the code for the nine remaining digits? Does your reading agree with the numerals in the address?

Can you figure out the system used by the inventors of the postal code? Find an envelope with a postal code printed on it. Can you read it? You may want to rewrite it using larger marks so that you can read it more easily.

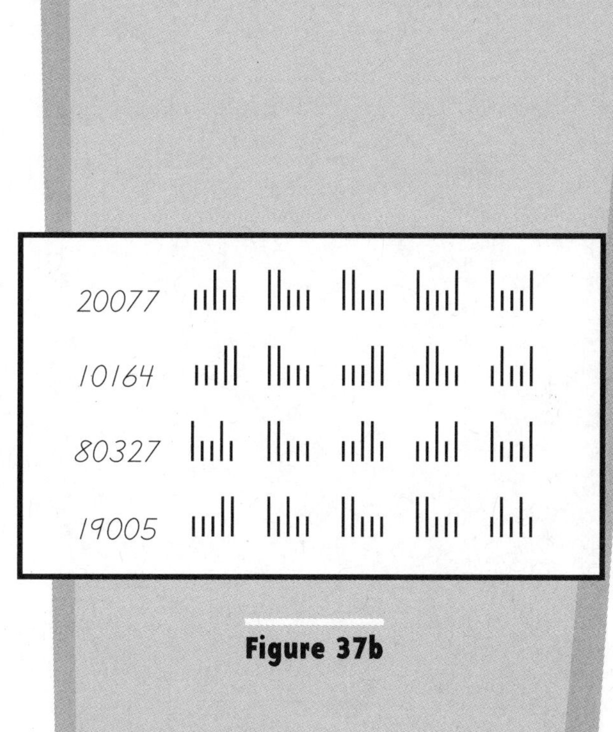

Figure 37b

6

Puzzles Without Numbers

Many puzzles have no numbers at all. They require logical thinking. You have to use your brain to figure out patterns.

This section has two kinds of puzzles. The first type is about crossing the river with different kinds of cargo—people, animals, or food. Some of these people, animals, or food cannot be left with the others, but the boat is too small for everything to fit into it at once.

The second type of puzzle is called a network puzzle and it comes from two different groups of people in Africa. Both groups of people told stories and made drawings in the sand but for different reasons. You will probably make your drawings, or networks, with paper and pencil. Some of the puzzles are a real challenge!

Crossing the River in the Sea Islands

Jonah stood on the bank of the river and wondered what to do. Next to him stood a fox. Nearby was a duck and a bag of corn. He had to row them all across the river before nightfall. But his boat was too small to hold everything. It could carry only two things besides Jonah.

Jonah would have to leave one thing behind. But if he left the fox with the duck on the other side of the river, the fox would soon make a meal of the bird. He couldn't leave the duck with the corn because the duck would eat the corn.

Jonah knew that he must make more than one trip. How could he get the fox, the duck, and the corn across the river safely?

This puzzle was told by African Americans living in the Sea Islands off the coast of South Carolina. For more than one thousand years people have told "crossing the river" puzzles. Probably they really had to figure out a way to cross the river with their load. They made a puzzle out of a real task. People changed the names of the objects to suit their own cultures and to make the puzzle more interesting.

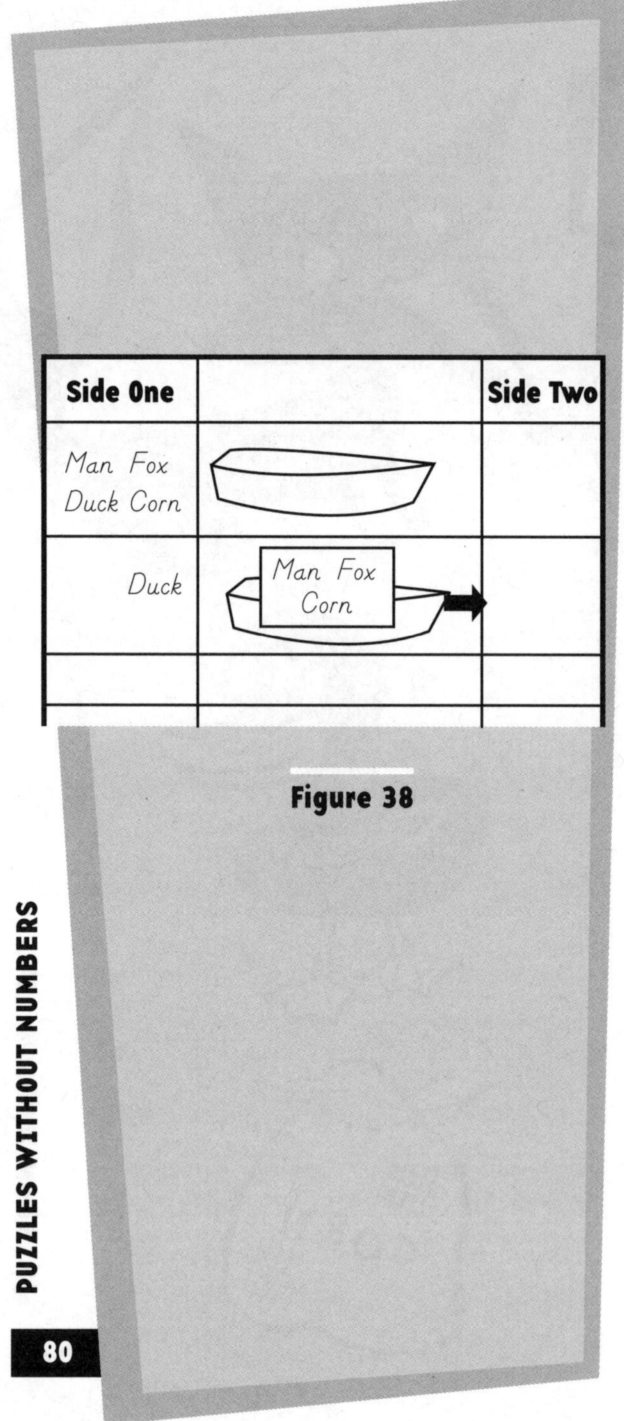

Figure 38

SOLVING THE PUZZLE

One way to solve this puzzle is to act it out with three other people. Each of you wears a sign showing which character you are playing. First discuss a plan of action, then see whether it works. If not, try another way to row all the objects safely across the river.

Another way to work out a solution is to write the name or draw a picture of each character on a bottle cap or piece of cardboard. Use a jar lid as the boat. Copy this diagram and finish it, to show how many trips Jonah had to make. **Figure 38**

Is there more than one way to solve the puzzle? You may check your answers in Chapter 10.

CHANGING THE RULES

Suppose that the boat can carry two items besides Jonah, but no two objects can be left alone together. Plan how he manages to get all the objects to the other side of the river. How many trips must he make?

Crossing the River in Liberia

Here is one way they tell the crossing-the-river puzzle in Liberia, a country in West Africa.

A man has a leopard, a goat, and a bundle of cassava leaves. He must get them all across the river, but his boat can carry only one object besides the man himself. If he leaves the goat with the leopard, the goat will soon be eaten. He cannot leave the goat with the cassava leaves because the goat will make a meal of them.

What is the fewest number of trips that the man must make to get all three objects across the river? Can it be done in seven trips? How many different plans can you think of? You may check your answers in Chapter 10.

Crossing the River with Jealous Husbands from Kenya

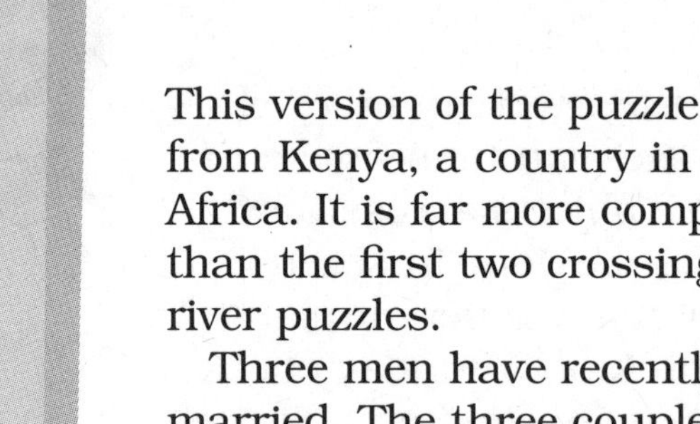

This version of the puzzle comes from Kenya, a country in East Africa. It is far more complicated than the first two crossing-the-river puzzles.

Three men have recently married. The three couples are going to the market across the river. There is only one boat, and it can hold only two people. But no man will leave his wife with another man, either in the boat or on shore. Fortunately, all three men and all three women can row.

Show how they all get across. They will need to make at least eleven trips if a wife cannot be without her husband but with another man as they transfer between boat and shore. You may want to ask a grown-up to work on the puzzle with you. You may check your answers in Chapter 10.

Crossing the River in Colonial America

I was looking through Wingate's *A Treatise of Common Arithmetic*, a book used in schools in the American colonies more than two hundred years ago. There I found two river-crossing puzzles. One was like the puzzle from Liberia, but with different characters. A farmer had to carry a fox, a goose, and a peck of corn across the river. His boat could hold only one object besides the man himself. He couldn't leave the fox with the goose, or the goose with the corn. How many trips did he make?

The second riddle was a real surprise. Here is the exact wording that I read in the book:

Three jealous husbands with their wives, being ready to pass by night over a river, do find at the riverside a boat which can carry but two persons at once, and for want of a waterman they are necessitated to row themselves over the river at several times. The question is, how those six persons shall pass two by two, so that none of the three wives may be found in the company of one or two men, unless her husband be present?

Here was the same puzzle about the jealous husbands that we found in Kenya!

The Snake & The Swallow's Nest from Angola

Figure 39a

Figure 39b

Word was out. Grandfather was about to tell a story and draw a *lusona*, a sand drawing, to illustrate it. The children hurried to the big shade tree and formed a circle around the old man. When they were all seated, grandfather cleared a space on the ground in front of him. With two fingers he made a pattern of dots in the sand. **Figure 39a**

Then he began to tell the story. As he was talking, he traced this pattern in the sand with his index finger. **Figure 39b**

A swallow built her nest between the four branches of a tree. A snake heard the little birds cheeping and decided to get a look at them. He glided close to the nest and went around the first branch. He glided on, went around the second branch, then the third and the fourth. Now he was back at his starting point. He kept going round and round the four branches over the next few days. One day he didn't hear the little birds and he decided to see what happened. When he finally went into the nest, he found it empty.

THINGS TO THINK ABOUT AND DO

Why did the snake want to find the nest? Why couldn't he go into it? Where were the little birds when the snake finally went into the nest?

On a sheet of paper, draw the pattern of dots. Then draw the path of the snake as it went around the four branches. Don't lift your pencil from the paper or retrace a line. After you have practiced drawing the path, tell the story to your friend or your little sister or brother as you draw the *lusona*.

The Chokwe Storytellers from Angola

The Chokwe people live in the northwestern part of Angola, a country in southwest Africa. Before the time of radio, television, and schools, children would learn about the ways of their people from the older folks. When work was done, they would meet around the fire or under the shade of a large tree. Children learned about their history, how to get along well with other people, and how animals behaved. As the elder told the story, he would draw *sona*, patterns in the sand. A single drawing was a *lusona*. We call such patterns "networks." A network is a system of lines that connect points. Think about TV networks, telephone networks, networks of streets and highways, and the Internet. Networks surround us!

First the storyteller would make a pattern of dots in the sand to guide him. Then he drew the lusona in a continuous line as he spoke. He never lifted his finger from the sand, and he never stopped talking as he drew the lusona.

A RIDDLE

This lusona is a riddle. First the storyteller made this pattern of dots. **Figure 40a**

Then he drew this figure around the dots. **Figure 40b**

Can you guess what it is? Here are some hints. It can send messages; it can keep the rhythm for dancing; and the top and bottom are covered with skins.

AN ANIMAL STORY

Another storyteller was telling children about an antelope that was running away from a leopard. The antelope left marks on the ground as it ran. Here is one paw mark. **Figure 40c**

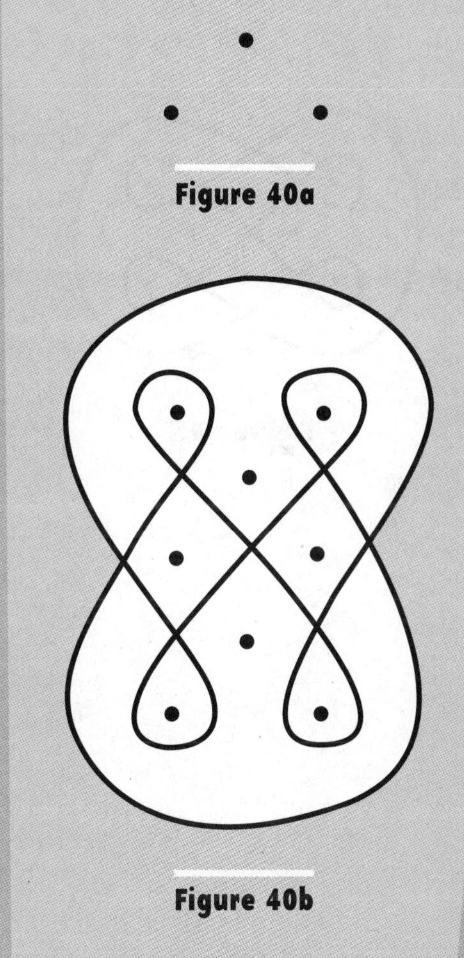

Figure 40a

Figure 40b

Figure 40c

MATERIALS

- **Sheet of paper**
- **Pencil**

THINGS TO THINK ABOUT AND DO

Compare the two sona. How are they the same? How are they different?

The answer to the riddle is a two-headed drum. Skins are stretched across the top and the bottom. Does the drawing look like a drum? Does the second drawing look like a paw mark?

Place a thin sheet of paper over the lusona. Using a pencil, trace lightly over the pattern that shows through the paper. Try to trace without lifting your pencil from the paper or going over a line more than once. You may cross a line.

On a separate sheet of paper, draw the pattern of dots. Then copy the network without lifting your pencil from the paper or retracing a line. You may cross a line. Practice until you can do it well.

Decorations on the Walls from Angola

If you were to visit a Chokwe home, you might see sona drawings on the walls. Men, women, and even children enjoy making these patterns. Here are some sona that you might find on the walls. **Figure 41**

MATERIALS

- **Sheet of paper**
- **Pencil**

THINGS TO DO

Lay a thin sheet of paper over a lusona so that you can see the pattern. Trace it lightly in pencil.

Draw some or all of the sona on a separate sheet of paper without lifting your pencil from the paper. First make the pattern of dots. Work in pencil, so that you can erase any lines that don't come out right. Then go over the lines with a marker or pen.

Make up a story to go with a lusona and tell it to a friend as you draw.

Draw four or five kumbi birds in flight.

Make up your own lusona to go with a story. Write the story and draw the lusona. You and your friends can make a book of stories and riddles, with sona to illustrate them.

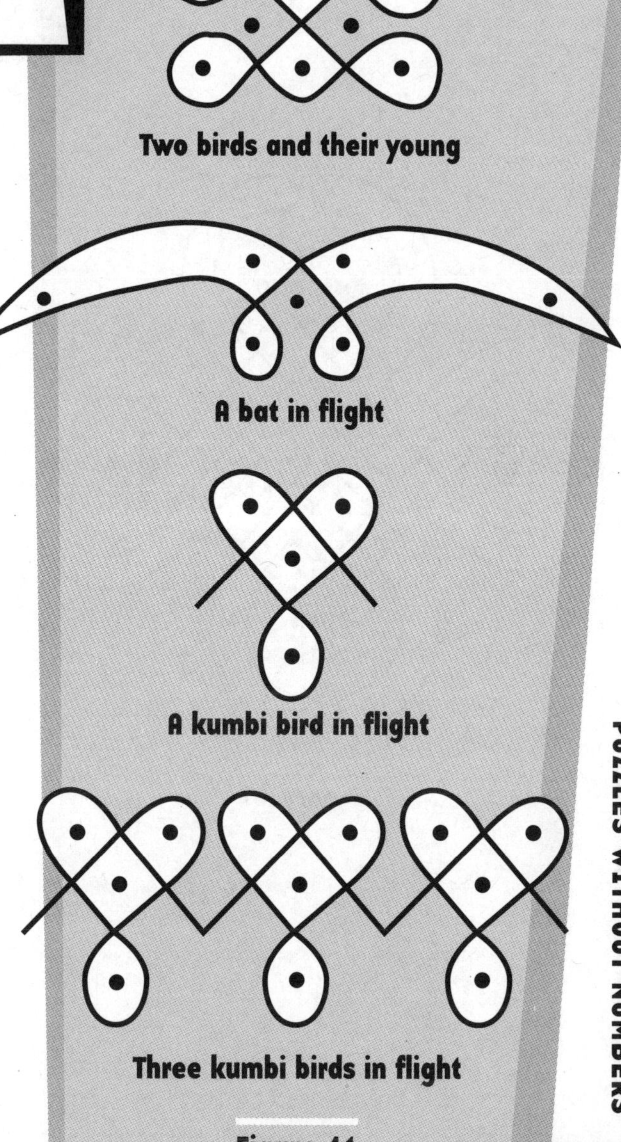

Figure 41

How the World Began from Angola

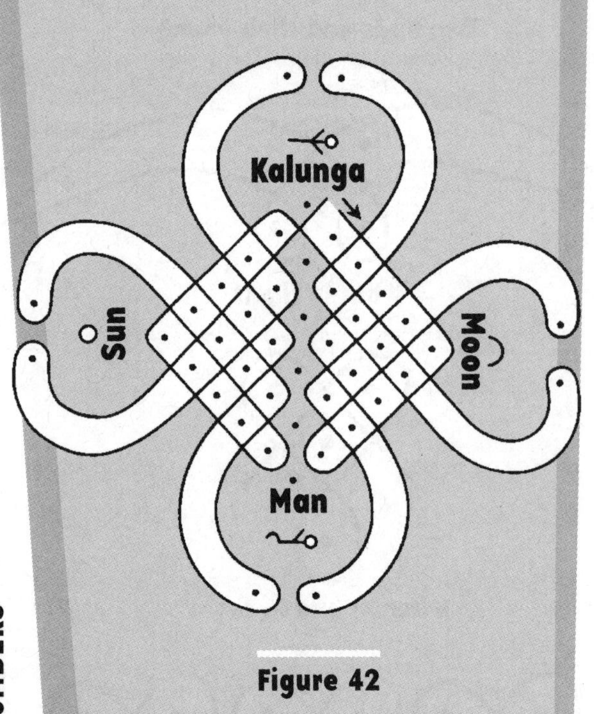

Figure 42

Most sona are larger and more complicated than those in this book. Here is the story about the beginning of the world, and the beautiful lusona that illustrates it.

Once upon a time Sun went to pay his respects to the god Kalunga. He walked and walked until he found the path that led to Kalunga. When he arrived, Kalunga gave him a rooster and said, "See me in the morning."

In the morning the rooster crowed and woke Sun. Then Sun went back to see the god Kalunga, who said, "I heard the rooster crow, the one I gave you for supper. You may keep him, but you must return every morning." That is why Sun goes around the earth and appears every morning.

Moon also went to visit Kalunga. He too received a rooster, and it woke him the next morning. When he returned with the rooster under his arm, Kalunga said, "I see that you did not eat the rooster I gave you yesterday. That is good. You must come back to see me every twenty-eight days." That is why we see the full moon every twenty-eight days.

Man went to see Kalunga and was given a rooster. But Man was very hungry after his long trip. He ate part of the rooster for supper. The next morning the sun was already high in the sky when Man awoke. He quickly ate the rest of the rooster and hurried to see the god Kalunga. Kalunga said to him with a smile, "Where is the rooster I gave you yesterday? I did not hear him crow this morning."

Man was afraid. "I was very hungry and I ate him," he said.

Then Kalunga said, "That is all right, but listen. You know that Sun and Moon have been to see me. Each of them received a rooster, just as you did, but they did not kill theirs. That is why they will never die. But you killed yours, and so you must die as he did. And, at your death, you will come back to see me."

And so it is. Haven't the sun and the moon always appeared, just as in the days of our great-grandparents? But men and women will not live forever.

Figure 42

MATERIALS

- **Sheet of graph paper**
- **Pencil**
- **Markers or crayons**

THINGS TO DO

With your finger, trace the paths of Sun, Moon, and Man. The arrow shows you where to start. Follow each line as far as it goes before changing direction. First you will trace one-half of the pattern, then the other half. Can you trace the whole design without taking your finger off the paper?

Follow the instructions on page 86 for tracing the pattern and then drawing it. It won't be easy!

Many sona are even more complicated than this example. The storytellers learned to draw them from their fathers and grandfathers. Often they kept this information a secret from those outside the family. The people who invented these beautiful designs must have been very clever!

Children's Networks from Congo

Figure 43a

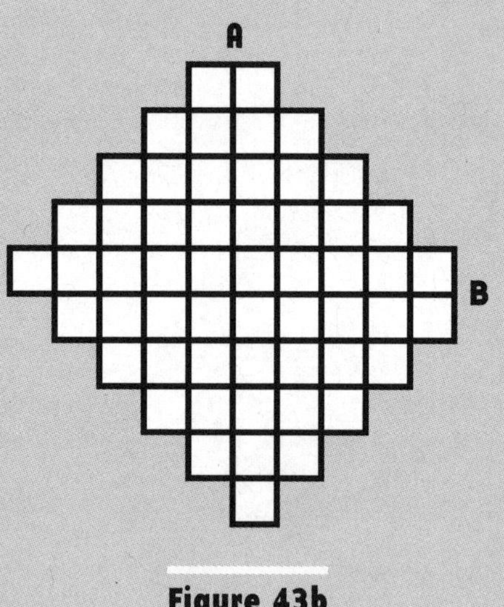

Figure 43b

Many years ago, Emil Torday, a Hungarian anthropologist, was visiting the Kuba people in Congo. He admired their beautiful woven cloth and wood carvings. They lived near the Kasai River, and many families made their living from fishing. **Figure 43a**

One day Torday came upon a group of children drawing patterns in the sand near the river. They invited him to sit down. They asked him to draw two designs without lifting his finger from the sand or going over a line more than once. The patterns in these networks are like the fishing nets that their parents made. This is one of those designs. **Figure 43b**

Torday wrote in his book: "I was at once asked to perform certain impossible tasks. Great was their joy when the white man failed to accomplish them." At last they showed him how to do it.

Let's look at the network. It has ten small squares in the longest row and the longest column. We'll start with small networks of the same type. Then we will build up to the larger ones.

Let's look at some simple networks. **Figure 43c** The first network has two small squares in the longest row. The second has three small squares, and the next has four small squares in the longest row.

MATERIALS

- **Sheet of graph paper**
- **Pencil**
- **Markers or crayons**

THINGS TO THINK ABOUT AND DO

Copy the smallest network in figure 43c without lifting the pencil or going over a line more than once. You may cross the lines. Are there special starting points and finishing points, or can you start anywhere? Try different starting points. Don't erase your work, even if it doesn't come out right. You want to find out what works and what doesn't work.

Following the instructions for drawing the smallest network, draw the next largest network, with three small squares in the longest row. Then draw the next one. The neatest method is to draw each line as far as possible before it changes direction. Mark the starting point and the finishing point of each network. What can you say about the starting point and the finishing point of each network? Can you spot them without having to try different points?

Draw a network having five small squares in the longest row. Continue with the larger networks, each one having one more small square in its longest row than the longest row in the network before it. Mark the starting and finishing points.

Draw the network that the Kuba children drew in the sand—one with ten small squares in the longest row. Be sure not to lift your pencil or go over a line more than once. You may cross the lines.

Color the squares to make beautiful patterns.

Here is a challenge. Draw a large network on colored construction paper. Then glue yarn of a contrasting color over the lines. You should be able to do the whole network with one long strand of yarn.

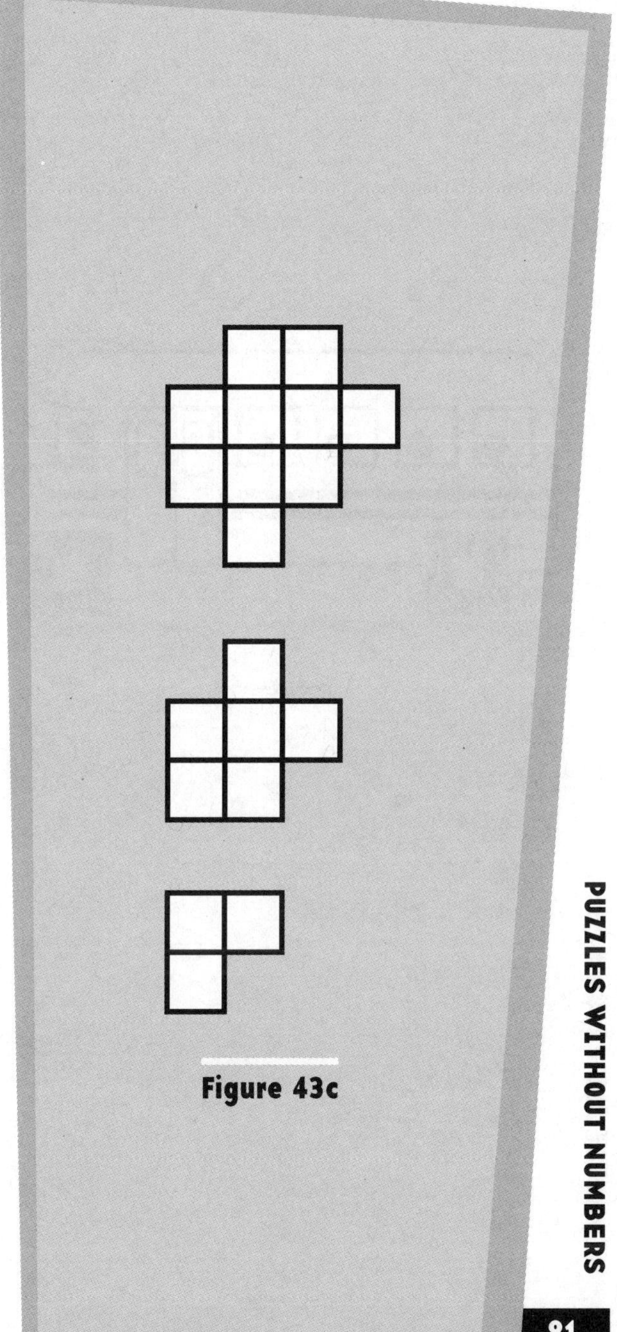

Figure 43c

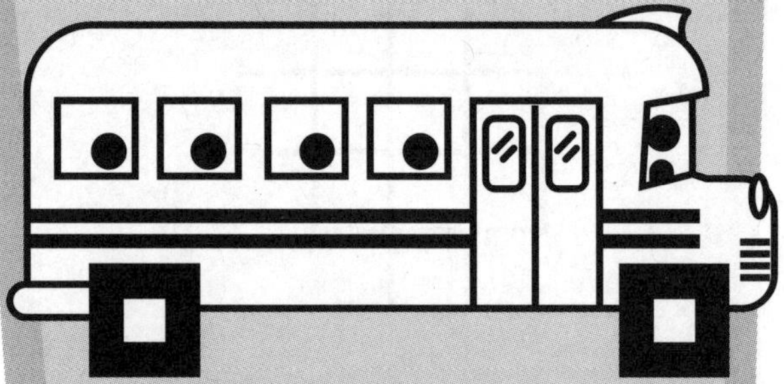

Figure 44

7

Geometry All Around Us

Look around you. How many round things do you see? Many things in nature are round. Look at the moon when it is full. In pictures, the sun is usually depicted as round. Earth and other planets are round, or almost round.

Many people have thought that the circle is the most perfect shape. No matter how you turn it, it always looks the same. Until scientists learned more about nature, people believed that the orbit of a planet around the sun was circular. Now we know that the orbit is an ellipse, a flattened circle.

Black Elk was a wise man of the Lakota people, Native Americans who live on the Great Plains. Here are his words, spoken many years ago:

Everything the Power of the World does is done in a circle. The sky is round, and I have heard that the earth is round like a ball, and so are all the stars. . . . The sun comes forth and goes down again in a circle. The moon does the same, and both are round. . . . The life of a man is a circle from childhood to childhood, and so it is in everything where power moves.

Why are so many things in nature round? For example, flowers are round in their overall shape. You have never seen a *square* flower, have you? Think about the way flowers grow—out from a center. Anything that grows evenly out from a center must be round. What parts of your body are round, or nearly so?

Many objects that people make are also round. Look at dishes, cans, jars of food, and other things in the kitchen. Try to imagine wheels that are not round! If you look around you, you will find many more round or almost-round objects. **Figure 44**

It is no surprise that people make round decorations. And when they invent designs that stand for events or ideas, they often use circles.

Some people build houses that are round. In this section you will learn why people build round houses, and you will read about some examples.

The Olympic Games Symbol

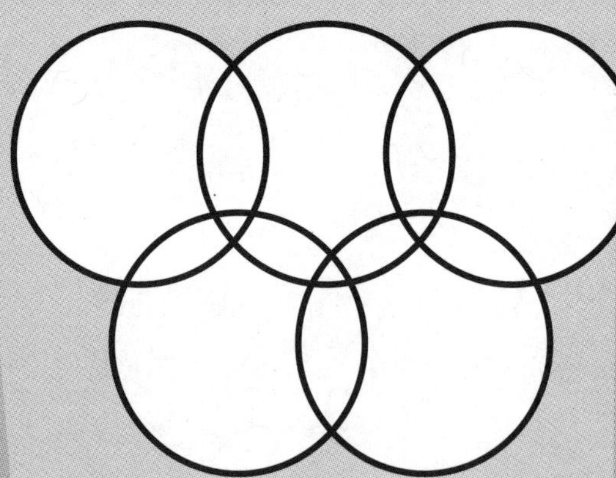

Figure 45

This is the symbol of the Olympic games. Symbols are designs that stand for an idea or an event. The five circles stand for the five continents. Most of the countries of the world take part in the games. They are held every four years in different countries. You can make an Olympic flag showing this symbol. **Figure 45**

MATERIALS

- **Sheet of plain white paper**
- **Pencil**
- **Compass**
- **Markers or crayons in 5 colors (black, blue, green, red, and yellow)**

DRAWING THE OLYMPIC SYMBOL

1. Copy the symbol in pencil. Use a compass to draw the circles. A jar or bottle cap or a coin may work as well.
2. Go over the pencil mark of each circle with a colored marker or crayon. Make each circle a different color.

THINGS TO DO

Now make another copy of the symbol. Use all five markers or crayons to color it differently from the first. How many different arrangements of the five colors are there? If you have a lot of patience, you may be able to find 120 different arrangements!

The Yin-Yang Symbol from China

The yin-yang symbol is Chinese. The symbol stands for the unity of opposites in nature. For example, light and darkness combine to form a union of opposites. Some think that the yin half is feminine and the yang half is masculine. Wetness and dryness is another example of opposites. What other opposites in nature can you think of? Here's how to draw a yin-yang symbol. **Figure 46a**

MATERIALS

- **Sheet of plain white paper**
- **Pencil with eraser**
- **Compass**
- **Ruler**
- **Marker or crayon**

DRAWING THE YIN-YANG SYMBOL

1. Mark a point in the center of the paper. Place the compass point on that mark.
2. Draw a circle.
3. Draw a diameter lightly in pencil.
4. Use the ruler to find the midpoint of each radius and mark it. **Figure 46b**
5. Change the opening of the compass so that it is equal to half the radius of the large circle. Draw a semicircle from the midpoint of each radius.
6. Erase the diameter you drew in pencil.
7. Color one-half of the yin-yang symbol.

Figure 46a

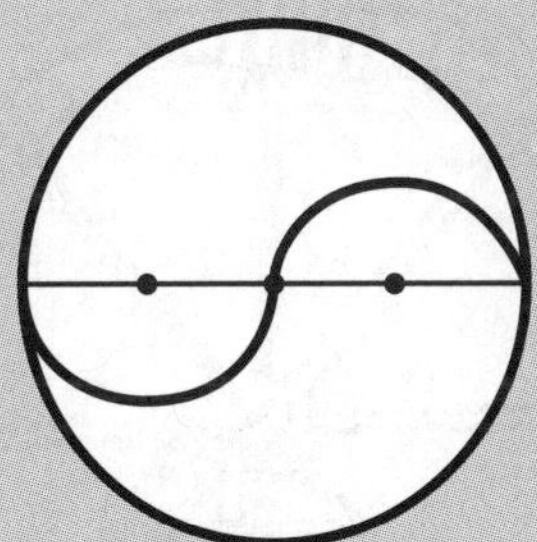

Figure 46b

Figure 47a

Figure 47b

The Dream Catcher

Native American

The Ojibwa people, Native Americans of the Great Plains, have a tradition they call *bawa ji guun ahbee*, which means "dream catcher." I learned about this tradition from a mathematics teacher at a university, the daughter of an Ojibwa elder. She also gave me the instructions for making the dream catcher. **Figure 47a**

The dream catcher was hung on a baby's cradleboard. Bad dreams were caught in the web, just as a spider's web catches and holds everything that touches it. Good dreams would slip through the web and make their way down the feather to the sleeping child. You can make your own dream catcher.

MATERIALS

- **12-inch (30cm) willow twig**
- **4 feet (1.2m) of waxed string or dental floss**
- **1 feather**
- **4 beads (1 white, 1 red, 1 black, and 1 yellow)**

If you cannot find all these materials, you may substitute others. Think about what would be suitable. You might use plain cord instead of waxed string. Instead of willow, use a thin twig from a different tree or bush. Soak it in water for a while to soften it before you bend it into a circle.

MAKING A DREAM CATCHER

1. Bend the twig into a circle and wrap the ends with a piece of the string.
2. Tie four strands of string across the frame, evenly spaced. Each strand marks a diameter of the circle.
3. Tie all the strands together in the center. **Figure 47b**
4. Tie one end of a two-foot string to one of the cross strands. This is the weaving string. Start to weave. **Figure 47c**
5. As you weave, wrap the string tightly around the strand in a figure-eight knot. Follow the arrows and the numbers in this diagram. **Figure 47d**
6. Tie a feather onto a short piece of thread. String the four beads onto the thread, and tie the thread to the center of the web.

THE DREAM CATCHER AS A SYMBOL

The circle is central in the lives of many Native American people. Here it represents the harmony of Mother Earth and nature. The string stands for the path of life. The beads are for the four directions. White is for the north, red is for the south, yellow is for the west, and black is for the east. The feather is for the effort needed to overcome the hardships of life.

THINGS TO THINK ABOUT AND DO

Why do you think the circle is so important in the culture and life of many Native Americans?

Write a story to go with the dream catcher. Draw a dream catcher to illustrate your story. Read the story to a young child or to a friend. You may also want to read the lovely book *Dream Catcher* by Audrey Osofsky.

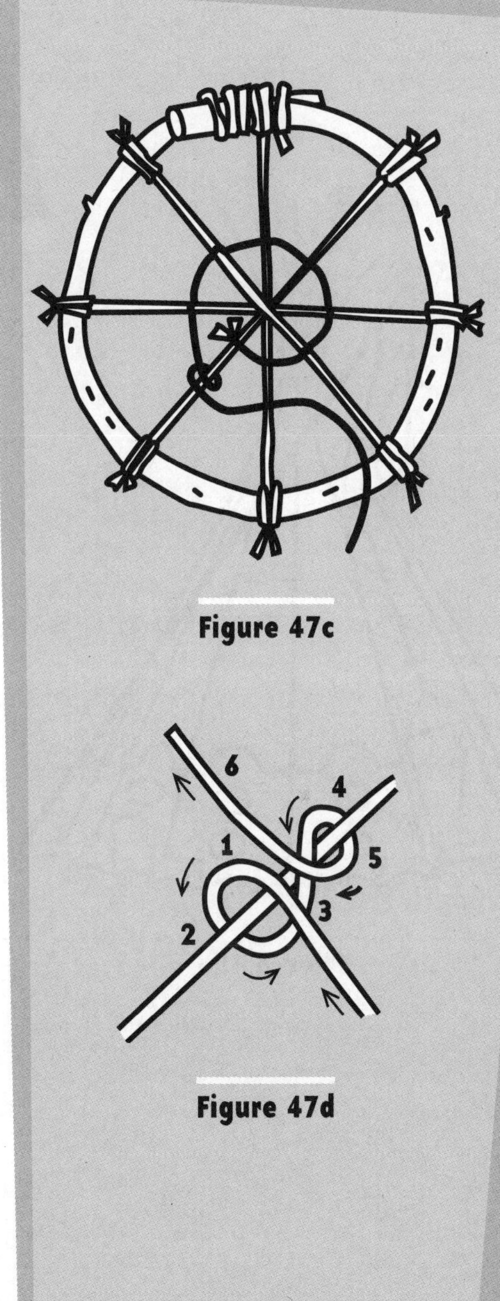

Figure 47c

Figure 47d

The Tipi Native American

Figure 48a

At the beginning of this section about circles, you read the words of Black Elk, the Oglala Lakota elder. The government had forced his people, the Lakota nation (also called Sioux), to resettle on a reservation. This is what Black Elk said about the way they had to live:

> *We made these little gray houses of logs that you see, and they are square. It is a bad way to live, for there can be no power in a square. . . . Our tipis were round like the nests of birds, and these were always set in a circle, the nation's hoop, a nest of many nests. . . .*

The Native Americans of the Great Plains were nomadic. They followed the buffalo herds as they wandered across the grassy plains in search of food. The buffalo supplied most of the people's needs. Every spring the women of the family made a new tipi of buffalo hides. When the people moved to a new location, they took apart the tipi and bundled it onto a travois, a kind of sled, along with their other possessions. Strong horses pulled the load.

The tipi is considered the most perfect tent. It is often thought of as the "good mother who shelters her children." The four main poles are called the grandfathers. They point to the four directions. To the east are the moon and stars. To the south are the sky and the mountains. To the west are the animals. To the north are the people. The pole to the north, like the people, needs the support of the other three poles. **Figure 48a**

Tipis faced east to catch the rays of the rising sun and to keep out the wind that blew from the west. The flaps were opened to let out the smoke, or closed to keep out the rain.

Today many Native Americans live in cities and towns, much like other Americans. They use the tipi mainly for ceremonies. You can make a paper model of a tipi. You may decide how large you want to make it, or you may follow the directions below.

MATERIALS

- **White, yellow, or tan construction paper**
- **Compass or bowl with 8-inch diameter**
- **Pencil**
- **Scissors**
- **Colored markers or crayons**
- **6-inch length of string**
- **4 1/8-inch dowel rods, about 6 inches (15cm) long**
- **6-inch (15cm) square of Styrofoam**
- **Tape**
- **Ruler**

MAKING A TIPI

1. Use this pattern as a guide. **Figure 48b** Lay the bowl on the paper or use a compass to draw a semicircle (half circle) with an eight-inch diameter. With a pencil draw semicircles for the opening, and "wings" to make the flaps. Cut out the tipi.
2. Draw a design on the tipi and color it. Red, yellow, black, and green are good colors. Fold back the flaps.
3. With the string, tie the ends of the dowel rods together. Set them up on the Styrofoam square. **Figure 48c**
4. Fit the tipi around the rods. These are the poles that support the tent.
5. Push one end of each rod into the square of Styrofoam. Then wrap the tipi around the poles and tape the edges together.

THINGS TO THINK ABOUT AND DO

Black Elk said there is no power in a square. What did he mean? Where is the power, in Black Elk's view? Do you agree with him?

Now that you have made a small paper tipi, you might want to make a larger one out of cloth or heavy plastic material. You might enlarge the pattern to make each measurement twice or three times the size of your paper tipi.

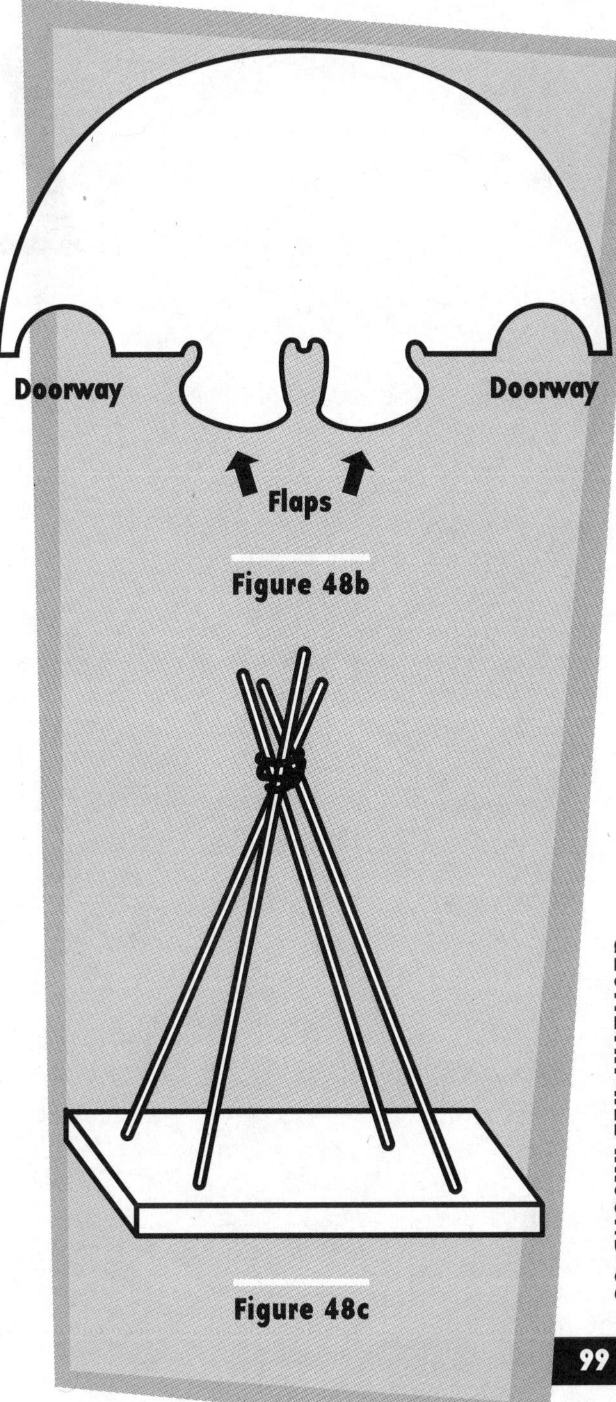

Figure 48b

Figure 48c

Round Houses in Kenya

Rodah and her husband lived in Kenya, in East Africa. They had just bought a small plot of land in the hills near Nairobi, the capital. The land had once belonged to Europeans, who had taken the best land for themselves and had set up enormous farms. When Kenya became independent from Great Britain in 1963, many Europeans left the country. Some of this land was divided into small plots and sold to the people of Kenya.

Rodah and her husband, with the help of their friends, built three small rectangular buildings—one for cooking, one for eating, and one for sleeping. When everything was finished, Rodah invited her grandmother to visit for a few weeks.

"Do you live in a house with corners?" her grandmother asked.

"Yes, we do," replied Rodah. Of course, a rectangular house has corners.

Her grandmother shook her head sadly. "I'm sorry, but I can't visit you. I have always lived in a round house with a center pole. There is no pole to support your house. Besides, I would get lost in such a house."

Rodah's grandmother had grown up in a house built in the style of the Kamba people of Kenya. The trunks of young trees were pushed into the ground in a circular arrangement. They were tied at the top to a thick post. Hoops of wood were placed on the trees. Then the whole structure was covered with thick layers of grasses, called thatch. A great deal of hard work went into the building of a Kamba house.

Cone-Cylinder Houses in Kenya

The Kikuyu people also live in Kenya, not far from the Kamba. Their homes are circular, with walls that are parallel. They are whitewashed to gleam in the sunlight. The roof is shaped like a cone and is covered with a thick thatch of grasses. This style is called a "cone-cylinder" house. Many different peoples build cone-cylinder houses. Some houses are tall and narrow, while others are short and wide. The style depends upon the materials that people find in their environment, the climate, the terrain (hilly or flat land), and the cultural and historical traditions of the people. You can make a model of such a house from paper. **Figure 49a**

MATERIALS

- **Several sheets of construction paper**
- **Scissors**
- **Tape**
- **Compass or bowl**
- **Pencil**
- **Brown crayon or marker, or clumps of real grass and some glue**

MAKING A CONE-CYLINDER HOUSE

1. The walls of the house are in the shape of a cylinder. Cut out a paper rectangle. Cut out a doorway. Tape the edges together to form a cylinder. **Figure 49b**
2. With the compass or the bowl, trace a large circle and cut it out.
3. Draw a radius in the circle. Cut along the radius.
4. Slide one edge under the other to form a cone. You can decide how steep you would like the roof to be. It should cover the walls and overhang a bit.

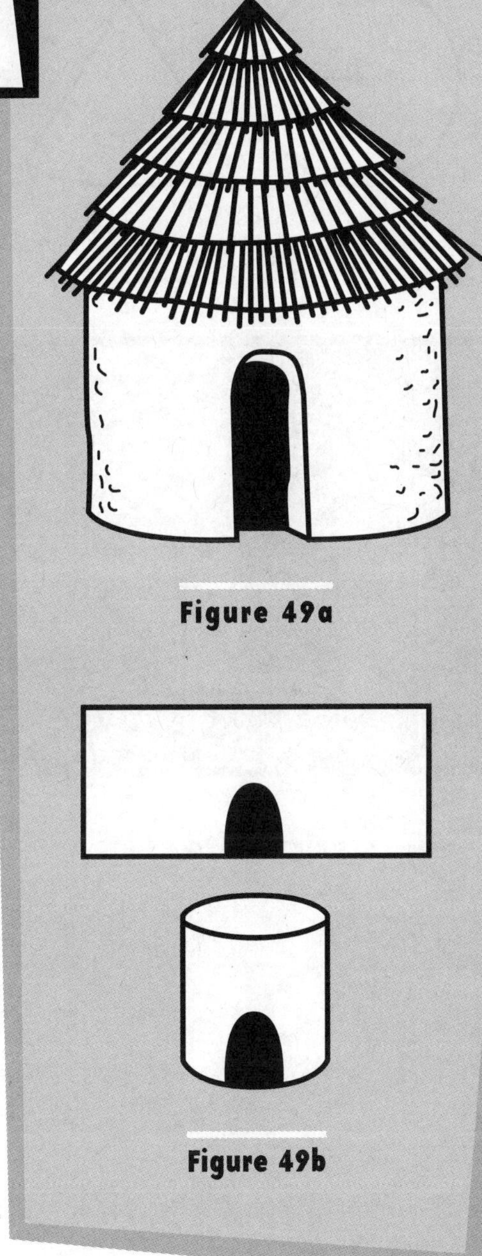

Figure 49a

Figure 49b

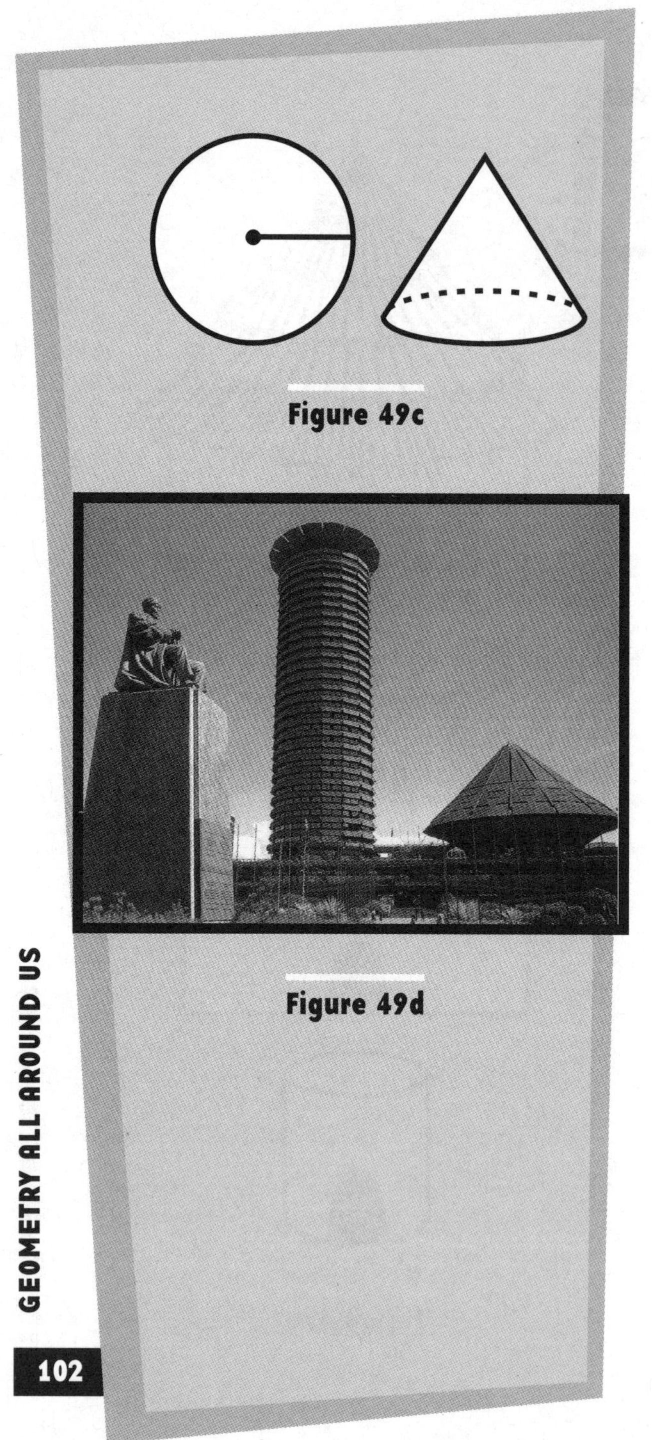
Figure 49c

Figure 49d

5. Draw brown grass on the roof, or glue real grass to the roof. Tape the edges. **Figure 49c**
6. Tape the cone to the cylinder.

THINGS TO THINK ABOUT AND DO

Would you feel comfortable in a round house? Why or why not?

You might enjoy reading *The Village of Round and Square Houses* by Ann Grifalconi. It takes place in Cameroon, a country in West Africa, and tells why some houses are round and others are square.

Experiment with several different styles of cone-cylinder houses. Figure out the measurements that will give you the style you have in mind.

Some people build the walls of their houses using sun-dried bricks that they make themselves. You can shape clay into small bricks and build a model of such a house. Place a cone-shaped thatched roof on the walls.

Some people who used to build round houses have now changed to a rectangular shape. These houses often have metal roofs. Can you think of reasons for these changes?

A few years ago the Kenya International Conference Centre was erected in Nairobi, the capital of the country. The main building is thirty-two stories tall. Are you surprised to learn that the shape of the building is cylindrical? Near it is a large, low building, also cylindrical, with a roof in the shape of a cone. To complete the conference center is a statue of Jomo Kenyatta, a member of the Kikuyu ethnic group and the first president of Kenya after it won independence from Great Britain in 1963. What factors do you think inspired the builders to choose these shapes for the buildings? **Figure 49d**

Look around you. How many straight lines, squares, and rectangles do you see? What is the shape of the room you are in? Are you sitting at a rectangular table or desk, on a chair with straight legs? Many of the objects that we manufacture have straight lines.

Tangram Polygons from China

The Tangram puzzle is fun for all ages. It was first mentioned about two hundred years ago in China, where it is played mainly by children.

The puzzle consists of seven pieces, called *tans*. Each piece is a polygon, a closed figure with straight-line sides. There are five triangles of three different sizes, one square, and one parallelogram. With a good imagination you can form hundreds of figures with these polygons.

MATERIALS

- **6-inch (15cm) square of heavy cardboard or Styrofoam**
- **Ruler**
- **Pencil**
- **Scissors**

MAKING A TANGRAM

1. Draw lines 1½ inches apart to divide the cardboard or Styrofoam square into sixteen small squares.
2. Draw the polygons as in the diagram. The numbers on the diagram tell you the order in which to draw the polygons. **Figure 50a**
3. Cut out the seven polygons.

THINGS TO THINK ABOUT AND DO

You will need to know the many ways the different figures fit together. Compare the polygons. Which triangles have the same size and shape?

How many small triangles have the same area as the medium triangle? As a large triangle? As the square? As the parallelogram? Try to cover each larger figure with small triangles.

Describe the angles of each triangle, of the square, of the parallelogram. Each angle of a

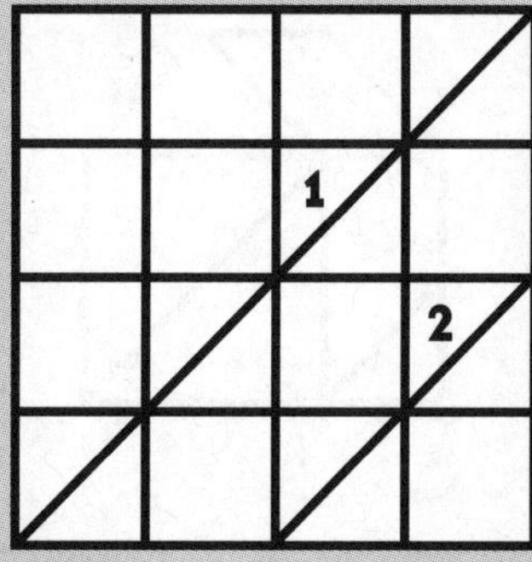

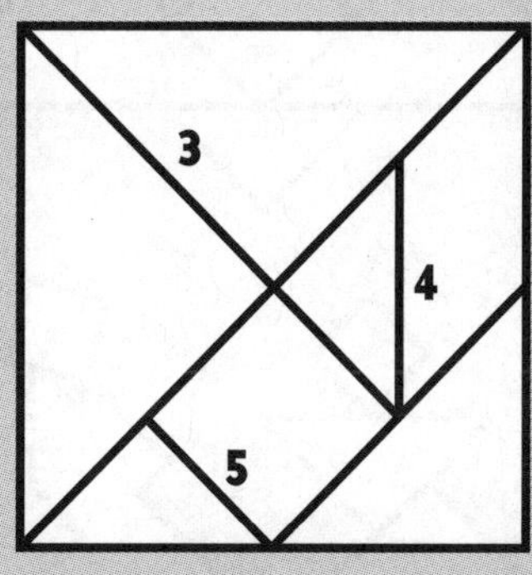

Figure 50a

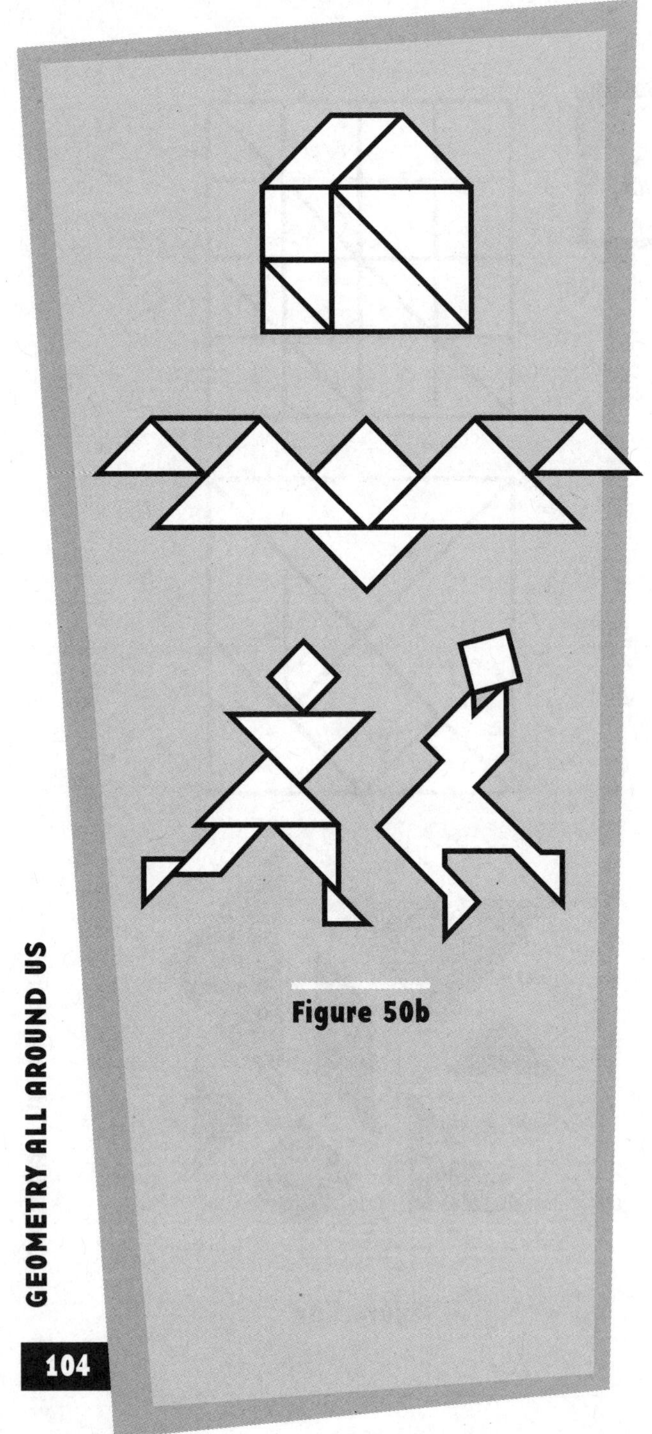

Figure 50b

square measures 90 degrees. Compare the other angles with the 90-degree angle.

Here are several shapes and figures made with tans. Copy each figure with your tans. **Figure 50b**

Invent a tangram figure. Lay it on a sheet of paper and trace it. Ask your friend to make a tangram figure like the one you drew on paper.

Read *Grandfather Tang's Story* by Ann Tompert. Grandfather tells his granddaughter a story about the fox fairies that can change their shape to avoid being caught. Write your own story and illustrate it with tangrams.

The Pyramids of Ancient Egypt

Among the Seven Wonders of the World in ancient times was the Great Pyramid in Egypt. It was built about 4,600 years ago for King Khufu and is the largest of the three pyramids that still stand on the Giza plateau. About 2,300,000 stone blocks, weighing a total of six million tons, had to be cut from the quarries and moved into place. Inside the pyramid are several passages and chambers. Each face of the pyramid is a triangle, and the base is a square measuring 756 feet (230m) along the edge. The height, 481 feet, is about that of a fifty-story modern building.

It is estimated that one hundred thousand workers needed more than twenty years to carry out the job. There were skilled architects, masons, accountants, scribes, stone cutters, and people who did the heavy work of dragging the stones up steep ramps. Most of these people were farmers who worked during the three months of the year when the Nile River flooded the plains and farming was not possible. What a tremendous amount of skill went into the planning, organizing, and building of a pyramid!

The five largest pyramids were built within one century. Later the Egyptians constructed great columned temples, as did the Greeks many centuries later. You, too, can construct your own pyramid. **Figure 51a**

Figure 51a

MATERIALS

- **Several sheets of construction paper**
- **Pencil**
- **Ruler**
- **Scissors**
- **Tape**

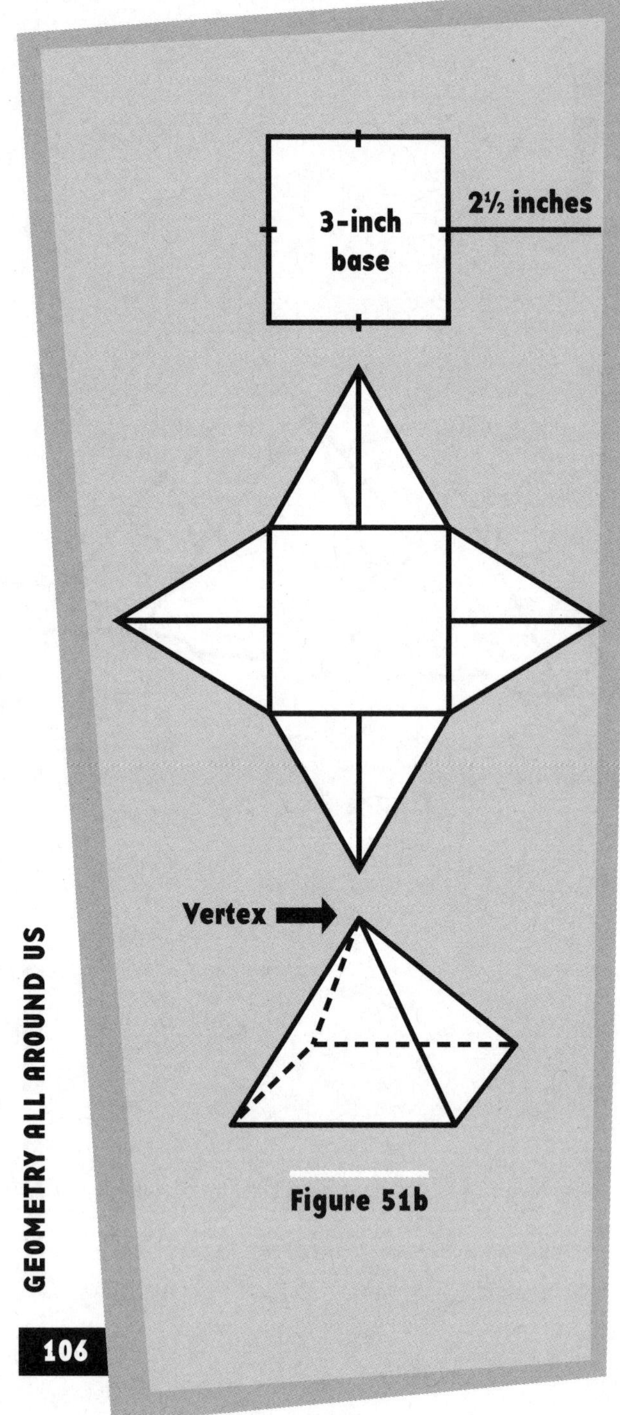

Figure 51b

MAKING A PYRAMID

Start with a small pyramid. Make a net like the one shown in the diagram. Measure carefully.

Figure 51b

1. Draw a three-inch (7.5cm) square.
2. Find the midpoint of each side.
3. Draw a 2½-inch (6.5cm) line perpendicular (at right angles) to each side of the square.
4. Draw the two sides of each triangle.
5. Cut out the net.
6. Fold the net so that the tips of the triangles meet at the vertex (tip) of the pyramid.
7. Tape the sides of the triangles together.

Now that you have made a model, try using cardboard or Styrofoam to make a larger pyramid. You might multiply the measurements above by two, three, or four, depending upon how large a pyramid you want to build. You may have to cut out each triangle separately and then tape the whole structure together.

THINGS TO THINK ABOUT AND DO

Why do you think the ancient Egyptians built such impressive structures?

Find pictures of the Egyptian pyramids and of the columned temples that they built later, especially the temple of the pharaoh Rameses II.

Read Anne Millard's book *Pyramids: Egyptian, Nubian, Mayan, Aztec, Modern.* As the book title tells you, many people have built pyramids. Among the most recent pyramids is the Transamerica building in San Francisco, made to withstand the frequent earthquakes in that region. It is 853 feet (260m) high.

The Parthenon in Greece

The Parthenon is one of the most beautiful buildings of all time. It was built in Athens almost 2,500 years ago as a temple to the Greek goddess Athena. It has forty-six columns altogether, and many marble sculptures. Sadly, this lovely building is in terrible shape due to the effects of pollution and war. Many of its sculptures, which are now called the Elgin marbles, were removed to the British Museum.

This classical Greek style of architecture was very popular in the United States in the early days of the republic. The Capitol in Washington, DC, and many other public buildings are good examples of this style.

The diagram shows one side of the Parthenon inside a rectangle. The ancient Greeks thought this rectangle was one of the most pleasing shapes because of the ratio of the longer side to the shorter side. They called it the *golden ratio*, and the shape was called the *golden rectangle*. **Figure 52**

What is the golden ratio? To find out, measure the long side and the short side of the rectangle. Divide the larger number by the smaller number. Is the answer close to 1.6? The longer side measures 1.6 times the shorter side.

THINGS TO DO

Make a picture. Cut a sheet of paper in the shape of a golden rectangle. You might make the longer side eight inches (20cm) and the shorter side five inches (12.5cm), or else double those dimensions. Draw anything you like. Draw a border around the picture like a frame. Do you like the shape?

Conduct a search. Try to find objects that are in the shape of the golden rectangle.

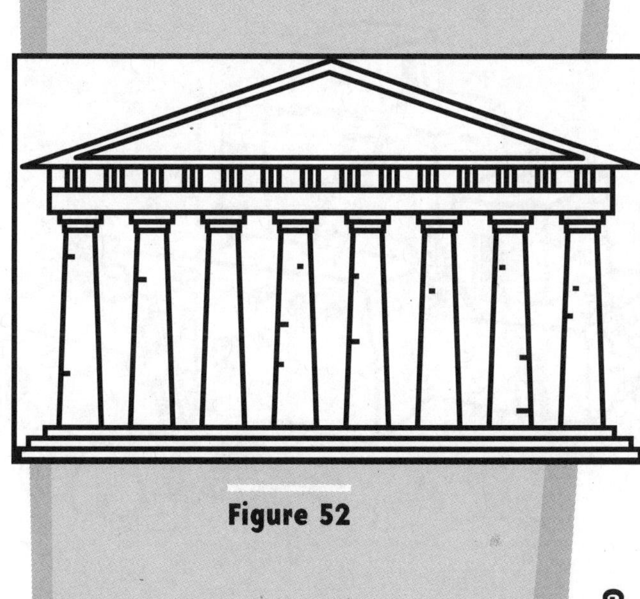

Figure 52

Pueblo Buildings in the U.S.A.

Figure 53

About one thousand years ago the Anasazi people built Pueblo Bonito in Chaco Canyon, in the region that is now the state of New Mexico. The Anasazi are the ancestors of the Pueblo Indians, Native Americans of the Southwest. Until the nineteenth century, Pueblo Bonito was the tallest apartment building in the United States. It had five stories and about six hundred rooms.

The word *pueblo* is Spanish and means both "people" and "village." The Pueblo Indians still live in Arizona and New Mexico and build their homes in the style of their ancestors. The building materials are bricks made of adobe, a mixture of clay, water, and straw. Then the structure is covered with smooth clay. This construction serves as air conditioning and is perfect for the hot climate of the region.

The Native Americans built one level at a time. To support the roof or ceiling of each level, they used logs, which you can see projecting from the building. The next level was laid on top of the one below, but with room for a landing or platform. Ladders helped them to climb to the upper levels. Build a model pueblo home yourself.

MATERIALS

- **Several boxes of different sizes**
- **Scissors**
- **Black paper**
- **Glue or tape**
- **Twigs or small round sticks**
- **Toothpicks and popsicle sticks**

MAKING A PUEBLO HOME

1. Arrange the boxes as in the picture. **Figure 53**
2. Working with each box separately, add doors and windows. You may cut the windows out or glue or tape pieces of black paper to each box to look like doors and windows.
3. For the projecting logs, make small holes in the boxes, insert the round sticks, and glue or tape them in place.
4. Glue or tape the boxes together.
5. To make a ladder, glue or tape toothpicks to two popsicle sticks.

THINGS TO THINK ABOUT AND DO

What shape is most important in the construction of the Pueblo home?

Read about the Pueblo people in *The Pueblo* by Charlotte and David Yue.

8

Designs & Symmetry

Figure 54a

What is symmetry? Look at your face in a mirror. The left half of your face is pretty much like the right side, except in reverse. Your left hand and your right hand are usually a close match, except that one is the opposite of the other. Your feet are usually a close match, too.

We say that the face has symmetry. The word *symmetry* comes from the Greek language. It means "same measure." We can also say that your body is *symmetrical.* Your two hands are pretty near symmetrical, and so are your two feet.

Symmetrical designs are very pleasing. They are often used as symbols or logos. A peace symbol hanging on a chain can be flipped over and it will look the same. Imagine that you draw a line down the center of the symbol and then fold the page along that line. The left half of the peace symbol would fit over the right half. The design has *line symmetry.* **Figure 54a**

This symbol stands for the talons of an eagle. **Figure 54b** See how sharp they are! This is one of the symbols on adinkra cloth of the Asante people in Ghana, a country in West Africa.

Give this book a quarter turn. The design looks the same. Now, turn it again, a quarter turn, and again. The design looks the same in four different positions as you turn this book. The design has turn symmetry. However, if you were to fold this design in half and then compare the two sides, they wouldn't match. This design does not have line symmetry.

The next few activities are about symmetrical designs and figures.

Look around you. You will find many objects and designs that are symmetrical. Some have line symmetry. Some have turn symmetry. Some have both kinds of symmetry. Make a list or draw pictures of some of these objects.

Figure 54b

Masks and Faces from the U.S.A.

Figure 55a

Here is a grinning jack-o'-lantern, a face made by cutting the outer shell of a pumpkin. If you draw a line down the center and fold the paper on the line, one half of the jack-o'-lantern matches the other half. The face has line symmetry. **Figure 55a**

Halloween is a time when people tell scary stories about ghosts and goblins and dress up in fancy costumes. These customs go back many centuries to early times in England, Scotland, and Ireland. The festival marked the beginning of winter, a scary time when it might be hard to get food and to keep warm. It was a time when the sun shone weakly or not at all and darkness came early in the day. The British colonists brought the Halloween customs to America. Their Native American neighbors taught them to grow pumpkins.

You can make a mask that looks like a jack-o'-lantern. You can wear it on Halloween or at any other time.

MATERIALS

- **Sheet of plain paper**
- **Sheet of orange construction paper**
- **Compass or bowl about 8 inches (20cm) in diameter**
- **Scissors with sharp points**
- **Pencil**
- **Black marker or crayon**
- **Tape**
- **2 lengths of string, about 12 inches (30cm) each**

MAKING THE MASK

First practice with plain paper to make sure you have the correct measurements so that the mask will fit you. Then make another mask with the orange construction paper. If you don't have orange, color white paper to look pumpkin-colored.

1. Using a compass or a bowl, draw a large circle about eight inches (20cm) in diameter. Cut it out.
2. Mark circles for the two eyes and a triangle for the nose. Cut out the eyes and the nose. To make sure that the mask is symmetrical, fold the paper in half and match the two halves. Are the eyes and nose in the right places to fit your face? If not, correct them.
3. Draw the mouth. Cut along the line between the teeth.
4. Use a black marker to draw the teeth. Add any other scary features you like.
5. Place tape on each side of the mask. Make a hole through the tape and tie one end of the string on each side. **Figure 55b**

THINGS TO THINK ABOUT AND DO

The Pilgrims ate pumpkins at their first Thanksgiving. This was a new food for them. How did they learn about pumpkins? Do you think they made jack-o'-lanterns? Make a mask or draw a picture of a sad jack-o'-lantern. How will you change any part of the face? Is the face symmetrical?

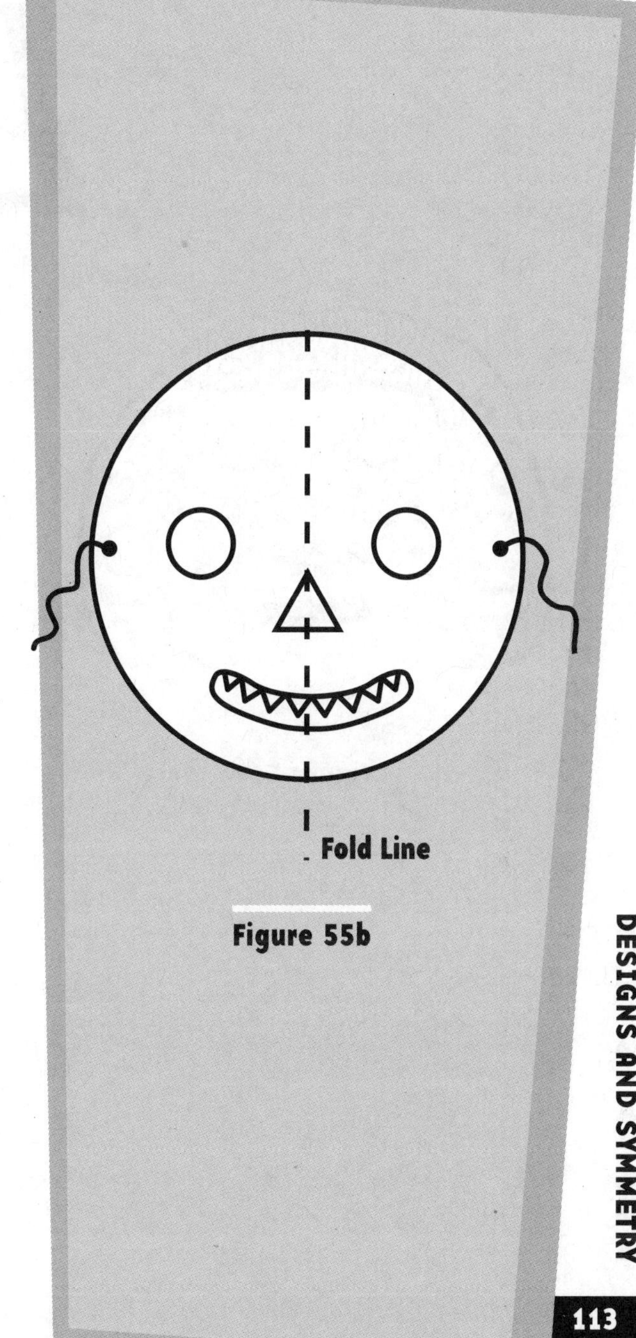

Figure 55b

Native American Masks

Figure 56a

Here are two Native American masks. One is an Aztec jade mask from Mexico. **Figure 56a** The other is a painted wood mask of the Kwakiutl people from the Pacific Northwest. **Figure 56b**

From about 1300 until 1520, the Aztecs controlled a large part of the land that is now Mexico. The capital was Tenochtitlan, a large city with a magnificent Great Temple and a Royal Palace. When Cortes with his band of Spanish conquerors came upon this city in 1519, they were amazed. They had never seen anything so large and beautiful. Decorations on the stone buildings were in gold and precious stones. Masks and other stone carvings adorned them.

The Spaniards conquered the city and all the Aztec lands. More than anything else, they wanted gold and precious gems to send back to the rulers of Spain. They built Mexico City on the site of Tenochtitlan. In a short time, war, disease, slavery, and hunger had wiped out most of the Native American population.

This jade mask was carved by an Aztec artist. Notice the symmetry of the face and the plugs in the ears. Wealthy Aztecs liked to wear earplugs made of gold or silver.

The Kwakiutl people live near the Pacific Ocean in the land that is now Canada. Their wonderful wood carvings appear on the house posts and totem poles. On special occasions they wear masks that may have been in their families for many years. These masks are made of wood that has been steamed and bent into shape.

Some Kwakiutl masks may hold a surprise. A mask may look like a serpent, but when the wearer pulls a string to open it, a fierce man's face appears inside. An actor telling a story would wear this type of double mask.

THINGS TO DO

Copy the Aztec mask and color it according to your own ideas. You may want to make an Aztec mask that you can wear.

Copy the Kwakiutl mask. The mask is colored blue, with red eyes and mouth and black eyebrows. Some parts may be the color of natural wood. Make up a story to go with the picture of the mask.

Figure 56b

Hopi Flat Baskets

Native American

Figure 57a

Here are three examples of baskets woven by Hopi women. The Hopi live in northeastern Arizona. Their name means "people of peace." Their ancestors, the Anasazi, wove such baskets more than 1,500 years ago. How do we know? Baskets have been found in the ruins of Anasazi homes. Now Hopi women weave baskets to hold bread and other foods. The most beautiful baskets are awarded to the winners of foot races.

Each basket has a different kind of symmetry. We will look for line symmetry and turn symmetry.

A design has line symmetry if you can fold it on a line so that the two halves match. Some designs have more than one line of symmetry.

A design has turn symmetry if it looks the same in more than one different position as you turn it. Suppose you want to hang this basket on the wall. **Figure 57a** Can you turn the basket so that it appears the same when you hang it from a different point? How many such points are there?

When you examine these baskets, remember that the designs in objects made by hand may not be as perfect as those made by machine.

Figure 57a. This design looks like a flower with four petals. It has four lines of symmetry. It also has turn symmetry, because it looks the same in four different positions as you turn it.

Figure 57b. This design is made up of circles. It has many lines of symmetry, an infinite number of them. "Infinite" means you can keep counting forever and never come to the end. The basket also looks the same in an infinite number of positions as you turn it.

Figure 57c. This design may stand for streaks of lightning. It has no line symmetry. It does have four different positions of turn symmetry.

THINGS TO DO

Look at the Hopi baskets. Find the lines of symmetry. Figure out the turn symmetry.

Draw several circles. Make up a design for each one, similar to the designs that the Hopi women made in their baskets. Try for a different kind of symmetry in each design. Color your designs.

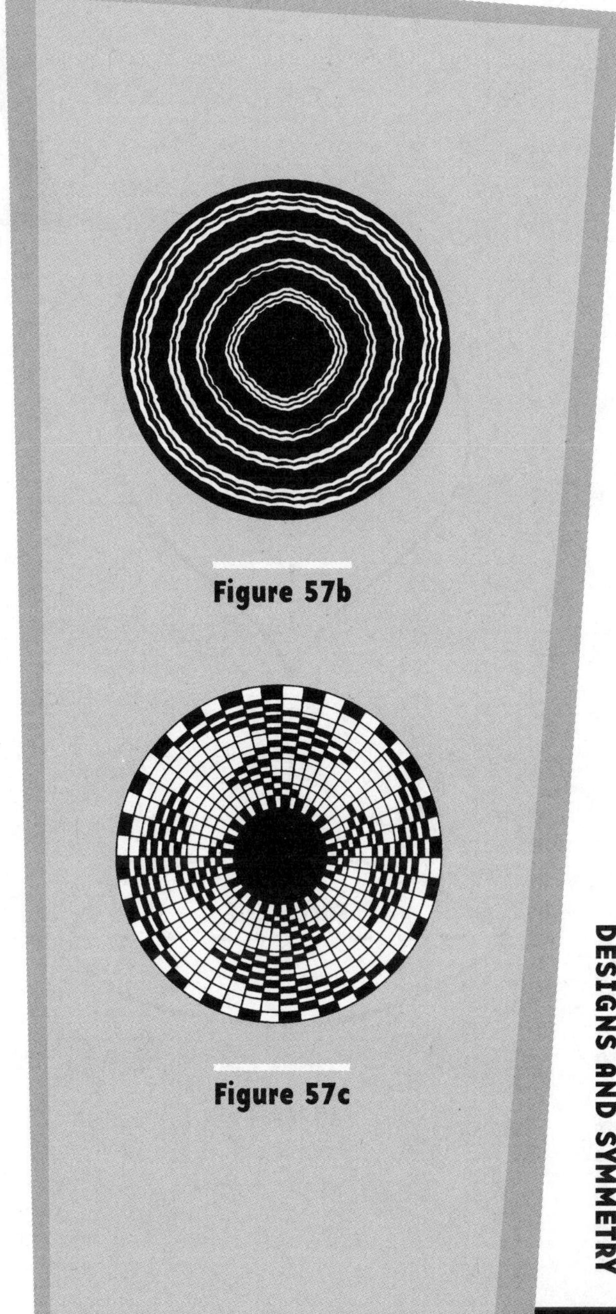

Figure 57b

Figure 57c

Pennsylvania Dutch Love Pattern from the U.S.A.

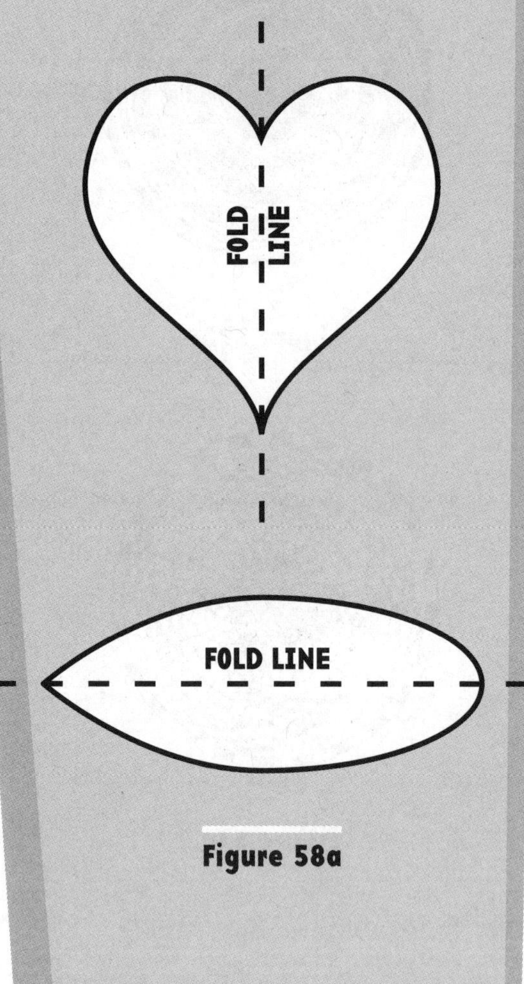

Figure 58a

You may have done papercutting already. Perhaps you cut out figures like these—a heart and a petal or a leaf. You probably folded a sheet of paper in half before you cut. One half matches the other half of the figure. Each figure has line symmetry. **Figure 58a**

This beautiful design comes from the German people who settled in Pennsylvania many years ago. They are often called "Pennsylvania Dutch." This pattern is called "Love." We know that a heart is a symbol for love. That's why we draw and cut out hearts for Valentine's Day. The Pennsylvania Dutch called such a symbol a *hex*. They hoped that such symbols would protect them from harm.

To make a copy of the Love pattern, you will cut out hearts and petals. Then you will glue them to a large white circle. The Love pattern has six petals. You may want to design your Love pattern with only three or four petals. **Figure 58b**

MATERIALS

- **Several large sheets of white paper**
- **Large bowl or a compass**
- **Pencil**
- **Red and green crayons or markers**
- **Scissors**
- **Red paper and green paper (optional)**
- **Glue**

DRAWING A HEX

1. Place the bowl on a sheet of white paper. Trace a circle around it. (If you have a compass, use it to draw the circle.) Draw a red and green border inside the circle. Cut out the circle.

2. Figure out how large to make the hearts so that they will fit in the circle. Fold a sheet of paper to make a pattern for the hearts. Trace the pattern to make seven hearts. Color them red and cut them out. If you have red paper, you can use it for the hearts.
3. Make a pattern for the petals. Trace it to make six petals. Color them green and cut them out. If you have green paper, you can use it for the petals.
4. Divide the circle into six equal parts, called *sectors*. You can do this by folding the circle in half, then in thirds. If you don't want to fold this circle, make a small circle of scrap paper and fold it. Then mark the divisions on the large circle. (If you have a compass, see page 56 for directions for dividing the circle into six equal parts without folding.)
5. Glue the hearts and petals to the white paper.

THINGS TO THINK ABOUT

Look at the Love pattern for line symmetry. Imagine that you can draw a line and fold the pattern on that line so that one half fits over the other half. Now find six different fold lines. (Pretend that the small heart in the center is not there.)

Look again at the Love pattern, this time for turn symmetry. Turn this book so that the pattern looks the same in another position. Find six different turn positions. (Don't pay attention to the small heart in the center.)

Figure 58b

Mon-Kiri Cutouts from Japan

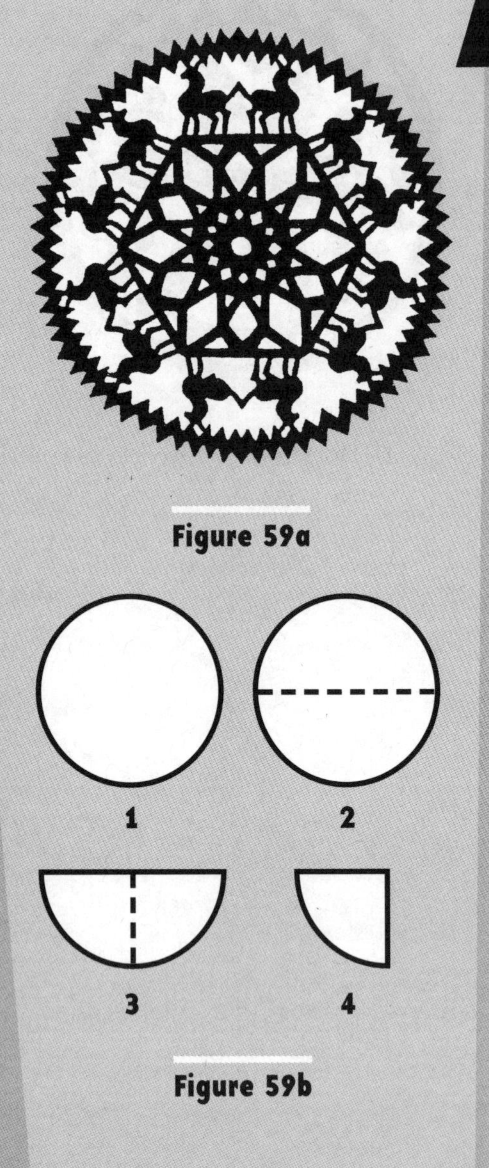

Figure 59a

Figure 59b

The Chinese and Japanese people have a long history of cutting complicated designs in paper. In fact, archaeologists discovered a Chinese papercut that was made about 1,500 years ago. **Figure 59a**

In the old days warriors would decorate their armor with these designs. Now the designs appear as decorations in books, on people's homes, and in many other places. Paper cutouts are often used in making cartoon movies.

In Japan this art is called *mon-kiri*, the art of folding and cutting paper to make designs. You can make a beautiful cutout in the style of mon-kiri. You might want to give it to a family member or a friend for a birthday or valentine.

MATERIALS

- **5-inch (12.5cm) circle of white paper**
- **Pencil**
- **Scissors**
- **6-inch (15cm) circle of black construction paper**
- **Glue**
- **8-inch (20cm) square of red construction paper**

MAKING A MON-KIRI CUTOUT

1. Fold the white circle in half, then in half again. **Figure 59b**
2. Along the folded edges draw several designs that will be easy to cut out.
3. If you like, draw a border pattern along the rim of the circle.
4. Cut out the design and the border pattern. **Figure 59c**
5. Glue the white circle to the black circle so that the black border is even all around.
6. Glue the black circle to the red square so that the margins are even all around. **Figure 59d**

THINGS TO THINK ABOUT AND DO

Look at the mon-kiri you made. Imagine that you can draw a line and fold it so that one half fits over the other half. Can you draw two different fold lines? These are lines of symmetry.

Place a finger on the center of the mon-kiri. Give the circle a half turn. Now it looks the same as when you started. The pattern looks the same in two different positions.

Fold another white circle as directed above. Then fold it again, so that you have eight layers of paper. Draw and cut out designs. Before you open the circle, can you imagine how many times each design will appear?

Experiment with squares and circles of paper folded in different ways. Draw and cut out the designs. Before you open the paper, try to imagine how it will look. Then open the paper. Did you imagine it correctly?

Look at the patterns you made. How many lines of symmetry can you find in each pattern? In how many different positions does the pattern look the same when you turn it about the center?

Another form of Japanese papercutting is called *origami.* Read the book by Eleanor Coerr, *Sadako and the Thousand Paper Cranes,* a true story about a little Japanese girl who was poisoned by radiation when an atom bomb was dropped on her city during World War II. She and her friends believed that if they folded a thousand paper cranes, she would become well. Sadly, she died before they had finished the task.

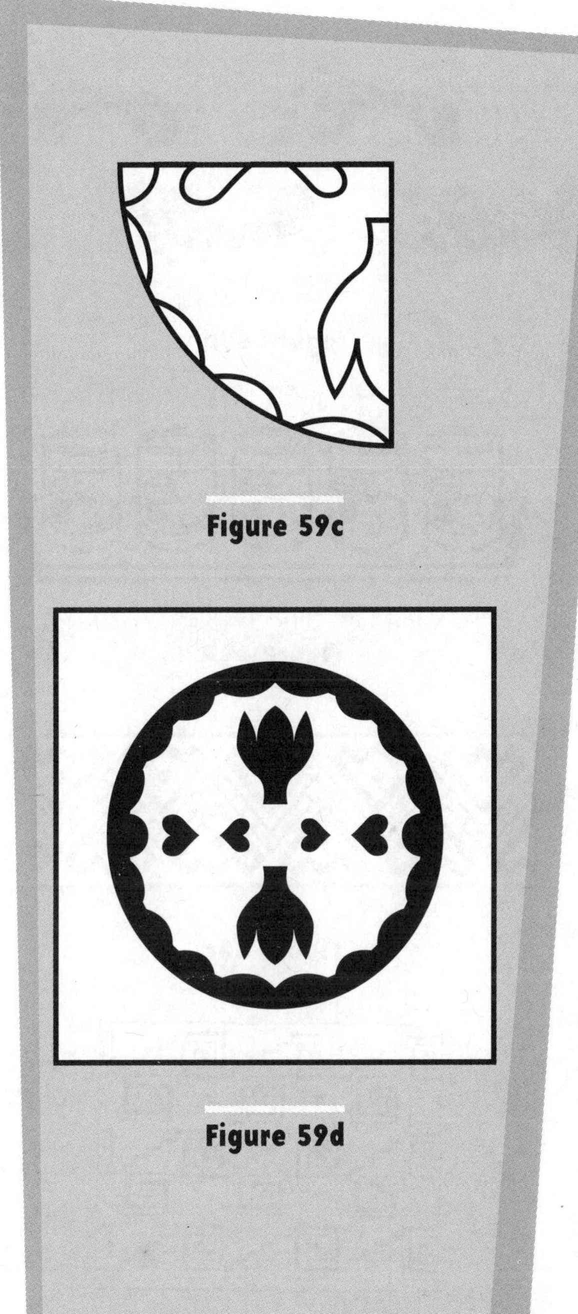

Figure 59c

Figure 59d

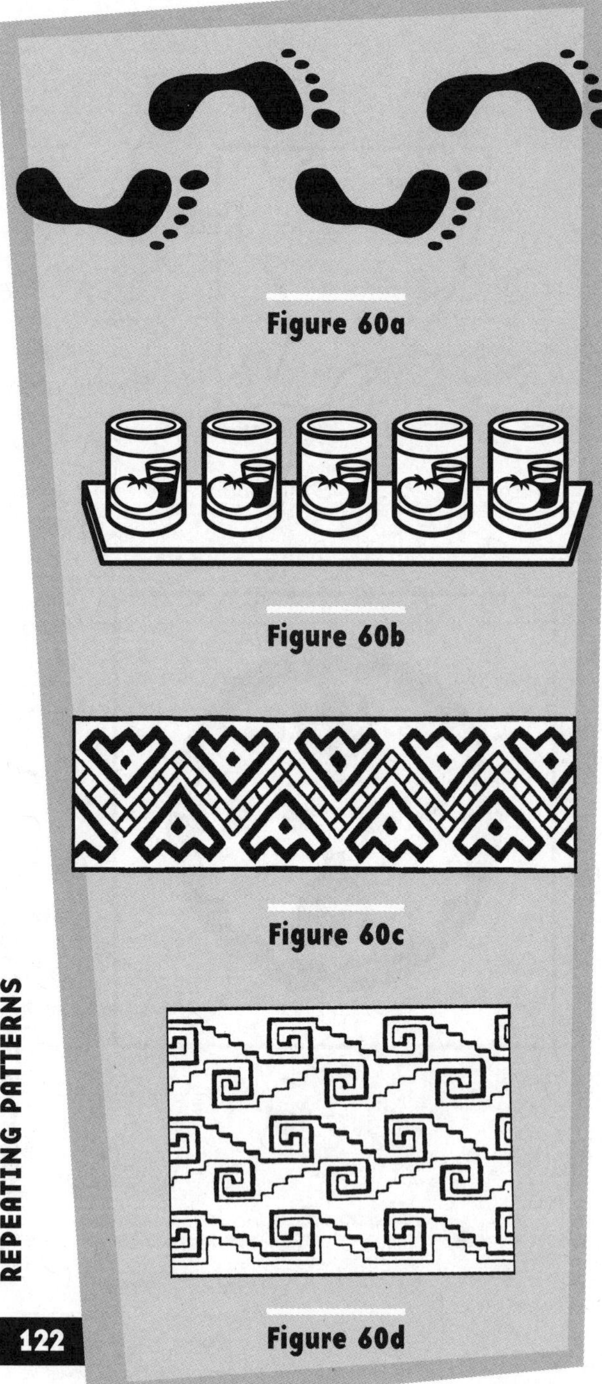

Figure 60a

Figure 60b

Figure 60c

Figure 60d

9

Repeating Patterns

When you walk barefoot in wet sand, your feet make a pattern—left, right, left, right. **Figure 60a**

In the food market, a row of cans, all alike, sitting on a shelf, makes a repeated pattern. **Figure 60b**

This border pattern is on a woven bag of the Ojibwa people, Native Americans of the Great Plains. The design is repeated over and over again, first one way and then upside down. **Figure 60c**

A design may be repeated to cover a whole surface. An example is this carved stonework in a temple in Mexico. The Zapotec people built it more than one thousand years ago. **Figure 60d**

Some repeated patterns occur in nature. Other patterns are made by people. Some repeated patterns are made as decorations. Others are useful, like the bricks in a wall and the tiles on a bathroom floor. Those described in the next activities are patterns people made for beauty.

Find other examples of repeated patterns along a line or row. Look inside your home and outside. Large buildings usually have rows of windows, all the same size and shape. Make a list or draw pictures of the examples you find. Look for examples of designs repeated over a whole surface. Make a list or draw pictures of some examples. Patterns in cloth and on tile floors are just a few examples that you might find in your home and your closet.

Yup'ik Eskimo Border Patterns from Alaska

The Yup'ik people live in southwest Alaska. They are one branch of the peoples called Eskimo or Inuit. Southwest Alaska is not as cold as the northern Arctic region. The Yup'ik people have never lived in igloos. Years ago they lived in houses that were partly below ground level. Today their homes are just like those of most people in the United States. They dress just as you do, go to similar schools, and use computers.

In cold weather they wear coats, called parkas, made of animal skins. Women decorate the parkas with borders of a repeated pattern. Each family has its own pattern, which is handed down to the children and grandchildren. They make the border by sewing small pieces of skin to a strip of skin in a contrasting color. The patterns are called *tumaqcat*, which means "cutout patterns." Here are some of the patterns they used. **Figure 61a**

Each pattern has a name in the Yup'ik language. The ending of the name tells you that it is "pretend" —"pretend windows," for example. The thick straight lines are "sled tracks."

Mary, a young Yup'ik woman, is very proud of the parka her grandmother made many years ago. The border has this design, repeated all along the bottom of the parka. The design has four windows inside a bigger window and mountains on both sides. Think how many tiny pieces her grandmother had to cut and sew! Every piece had to be placed exactly right. **Figure 61b**

Figure 61a

Figure 61b

MAKING A YUP'IK PARKA BORDER

Here are three different ways to make the border. Before you work with the materials, sketch the design and the pattern on paper. Measure carefully to make sure it fits together. You can make right triangles by cutting squares in half along the diagonal.

Cut-and-paste method. Choose one Yup'ik pattern to copy. Cut many polygons—squares or triangles or parallelograms—of construction paper. Glue them to a strip of paper of a contrasting color. Dark brown and light brown are good colors, as are black and white.

Tracing method. Cut one polygon of heavy paper or Styrofoam to use as a pattern. Then trace this polygon as many times as necessary on a strip of construction paper. Color your border.

Sew-and-paste method. Cut many polygons of felt and sew or glue them to a strip of cloth to form the border.

After you have made several Yup'ik borders, invent your own repeated pattern for a border, using polygons. First sketch it on paper. Give your pattern a name. Decide what you will decorate.

THINGS TO THINK ABOUT

Try to imagine how each pattern got its name.

Name the different types of polygons (shapes with straight sides) that you see in the border patterns.

Which patterns have squares? Find different sizes of squares in one border. How many different sizes of squares can you find in Mary's grandmother's parka? Which patterns have triangles? Which are white and which are black? Which patterns have parallelograms?

The Covenant Belt Native American

This belt, now in the New York State Museum in Albany, is made of thousands of wampum beads carefully sewed onto a strip of skin more than six feet long. It is called the Washington Covenant Belt because it sealed a treaty, or covenant, of peace between the Six Nations of the Iroquois and the thirteen colonies. It was a custom among some of the Native peoples to seal a treaty by making a wampum belt. It was regarded as a permanent record of the agreement. **Figure 62**

But the peace between the Iroquois and the thirteen colonies was broken. Here are the words of Chief Hendrick of the Mohawks, one of the Six Nations: "We will send up a Belt of Wampum to our Brothers the other Five Nations to acquaint them the Covenant Chain is broken between you and us." He was speaking to Governor George Clinton and the council of New York in 1753. The New York colonial government had taken eight hundred thousand acres of Mohawk land. That was the end of the friendship between the New York colony and the Mohawks.

Figure 62

THINGS TO THINK ABOUT

Look at the Washington Covenant Belt. It shows a repeated pattern of people. Do you see thirteen tall people? Why are there thirteen? What other figures are in the belt, and what do you think they stand for?

Examine the figures for symmetry. Is each person symmetrical? Does the left side match the right side? Is the house near the center symmetrical?

Notice that a small person has the same shape as a large person. We say that the two figures are similar—they have the same shape but different sizes.

Each wampum bead measures about $\frac{1}{10}$ by $\frac{1}{3}$ of an inch. One square inch of the belt would contain about thirty beads. The belt is about six inches wide and more than six feet long. Estimate how many beads are in the belt. Then check your estimate with the answers in Chapter 10.

THINGS TO DO

Design a belt to seal a treaty of peace with a friend or family member. Draw the belt and color it. What designs will you put on the belt? Will it have a repeated pattern?

If you have a computer, try to design a treaty belt on the computer.

African Patterns from Congo

The Kuba live along the Kasai River in Congo (formerly Zaire), a country in Central Africa. They became famous centuries ago for their wonderful embroidered cloth and wood carvings. In the British Museum is a carving of their king Shyaam aMbul aNgoong, who ruled in the early seventeenth century. In front of him is a game board for mankala. He is celebrated for bringing the peaceful arts to his people. He brought new crops, the arts of carving and weaving, and the mankala game they called *lela.*

Here are two border patterns from the art of the Kuba people. **Figure 63a**

THINGS TO THINK ABOUT

Look at each pattern. What is the shape of the design? Notice how the design is repeated again and again to make the pattern.

Look at the cloth pattern. Suppose you want to make a stamp of the design. What is the smallest design you need to cut into the stamp? Here are three choices. **Figure 63b**

Look at the cloth pattern again. Now you are going to make a stencil. You can use it to trace the design many times. You can flip the stencil over to the other side if you like. Which of the three is your choice for the smallest design to cut into the stamp? Does it make a difference whether you put your design on a stamp or on a stencil that can be used on both sides? Check your conclusions with the answers in Chapter 10.

Figure 63a

Figure 63b

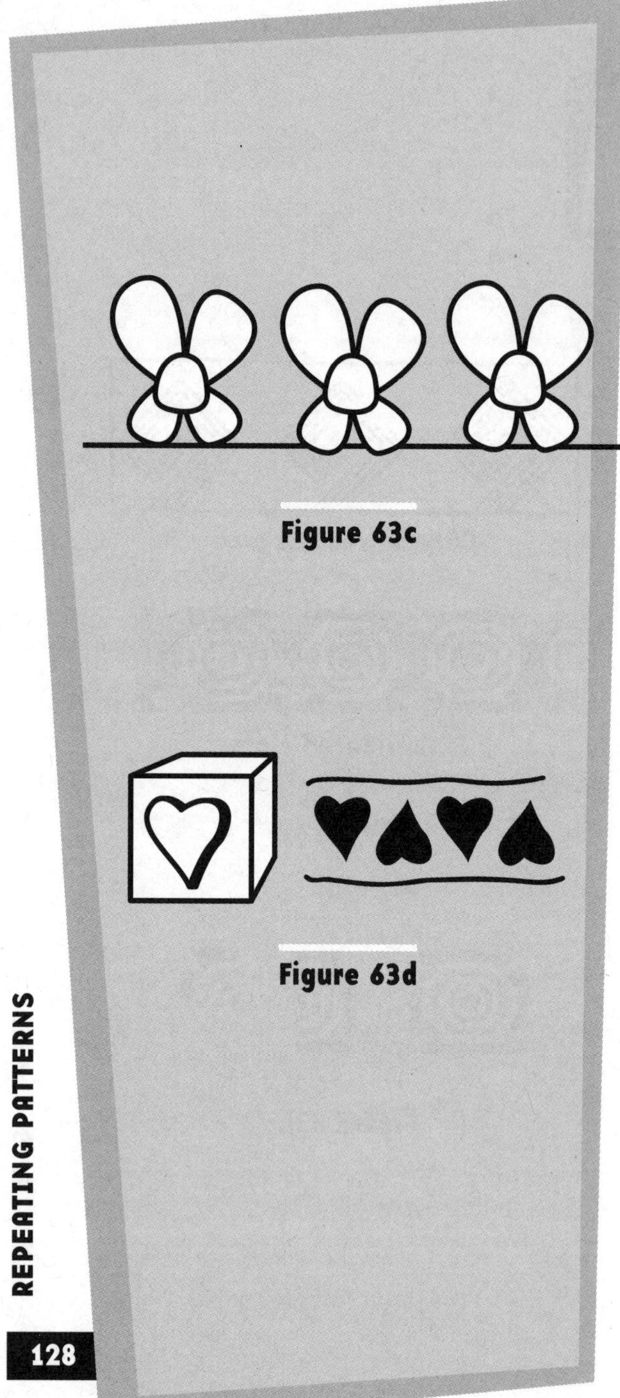

Figure 63c

Figure 63d

THINGS TO DO

You can make your own borders for place mats, book covers, and other kinds of decorations. Here are some ways to do it.

Tracing method. Cut a design out of heavy paper or plastic. Draw a long line on a sheet of plain paper. Trace your design on this line. Repeat it as many times as you can. Then color the design. **Figure 63c**

Stamp method. Draw a simple design to put on a stamp. To make a stamp, cut the design on the flat side of half a potato or on a sponge. Ask a grown-up to help you. Draw a track (two parallel lines) in which to stamp the design. Decide how you are going to repeat the pattern along the track. Use washable ink or finger paint. Then make another track and repeat the pattern in a different way. **Figure 63d**

Stencil method. Here are some instructions for making a stencil for a design that you will repeat to make a border. **Figure 63e**

MATERIALS

- **Rectangle of heavy paper or plastic, about 1½ by 2 inches (3½ by 5cm)**
- **Pencil**
- **Scissors**
- **Ruler**
- **Sheet of plain paper**
- **Crayons or markers**

MAKING A BORDER STENCIL

1. To make the stencil, draw a simple design on the rectangle. Cut it out.
2. On the plain paper, draw a track as wide as the rectangle. Divide it into rectangles the same size as the stencil.
3. Trace the design in pencil in the first rectangle on the track.
4. Decide how to place the design in the second rectangle. You might repeat the first rectangle, turn the stencil upside down, or flip it over. How many different ways can you find to make a repeated pattern with this stencil? Try as many as you can. **Figure 63f**
5. Color your border.

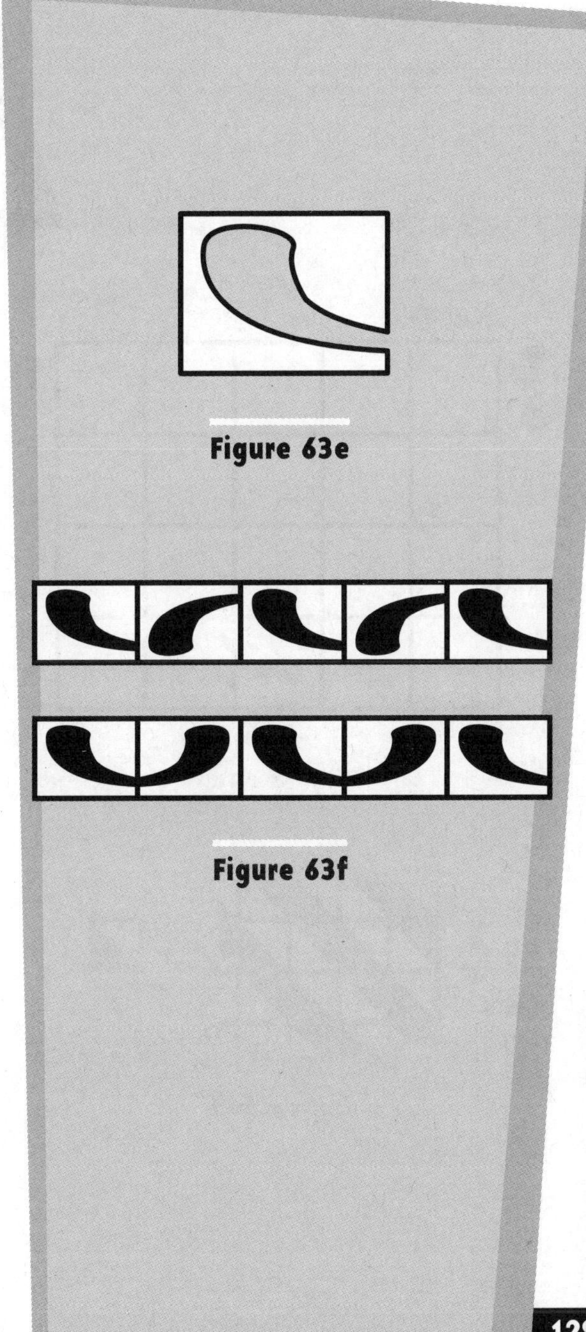

Figure 63e

Figure 63f

Patchwork Quilts from the U.S.A.

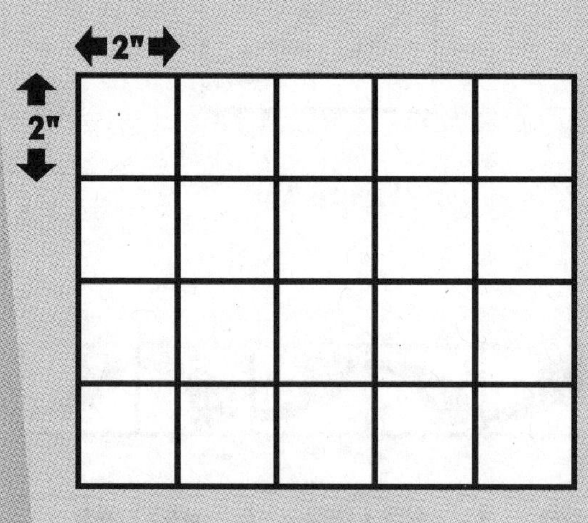

Figure 64a

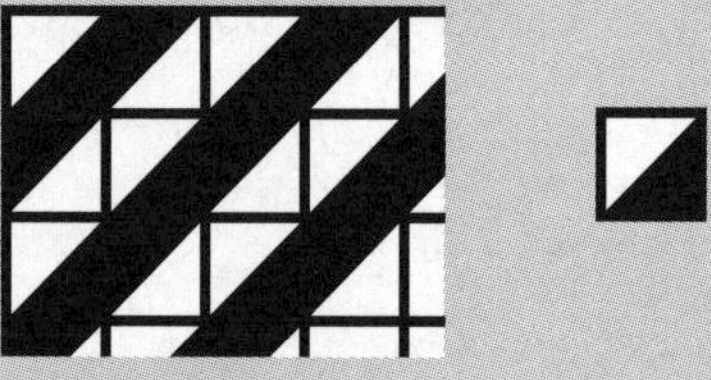

Figure 64b

At the time of colonial America and the early days of the United States, a great deal of work, such as weaving, sewing, and carpentry, was done in the home. In wealthy homes, servants and slaves did much of this work. Poorer people had to do their own work. Often these workers made very artistic creations.

One form of this art was quilting. Women who were stuck in the house arranged to get out every once in a while for a quilting bee in a neighbor's home. They would work together to make a patchwork quilt as a wedding gift or as a good-bye present to a family moving out West. Each woman did her bit of the quilt.

For many women, this was the only means of artistic expression. One woman wrote: "It took me near twenty-five years to make that quilt. My whole life is in that quilt." African American women sometimes bought their freedom from slavery with their fine quilts, which were often based on African patterns. Native American women also made quilts to honor the arrival of a new baby or for some other special event.

Today some quilters use the computer to design their quilts. And men as well as women are now quilting.

A fine quilt is a result of careful planning. Many patchwork quilts are made up of a lot of squares sewed together. Each square, in turn, may be made up of several shapes and colors. A quilt that has no design or pattern is called a "crazy quilt." A hodgepodge of things with no order may also be called a "crazy quilt."

For the squares, or patches, women and girls used leftover bits of fabric and pieces of worn-out clothing. Nothing was wasted. Only a very special quilt or one made for a wealthy home rated large amounts of new material.

Let's design a simple quilt with paper squares. You should cut out at least thirty-six squares.

MATERIALS

- **Pencil**
- **Ruler**
- **2 or 3 sheets of white or light-colored paper**
- **Marker or crayon**
- **Scissors**

MAKING A PAPER QUILT

1. Use the pencil and ruler to divide each sheet of paper into two-inch (5cm) squares. You should have at least thirty-six squares. **Figure 64a**
2. Draw the diagonals of all the squares. Color each half of each square contrasting colors. **Figure 64b**
3. Cut out the squares.
4. Arrange the squares in a pleasing pattern to make a large quilt. Here are some ways to combine the squares. You can rotate some squares a quarter turn or a half turn. **Figure 64c**
5. You may want to keep the best pattern. Copy it on a sheet of construction paper or glue the squares to the sheet of paper. Draw a border around it as a frame, or glue it to a larger sheet of a contrasting color.

You have just created a *tessellation*. A tessellation is a pattern that covers a surface completely by combining certain shapes. Your tessellation is made up of squares.

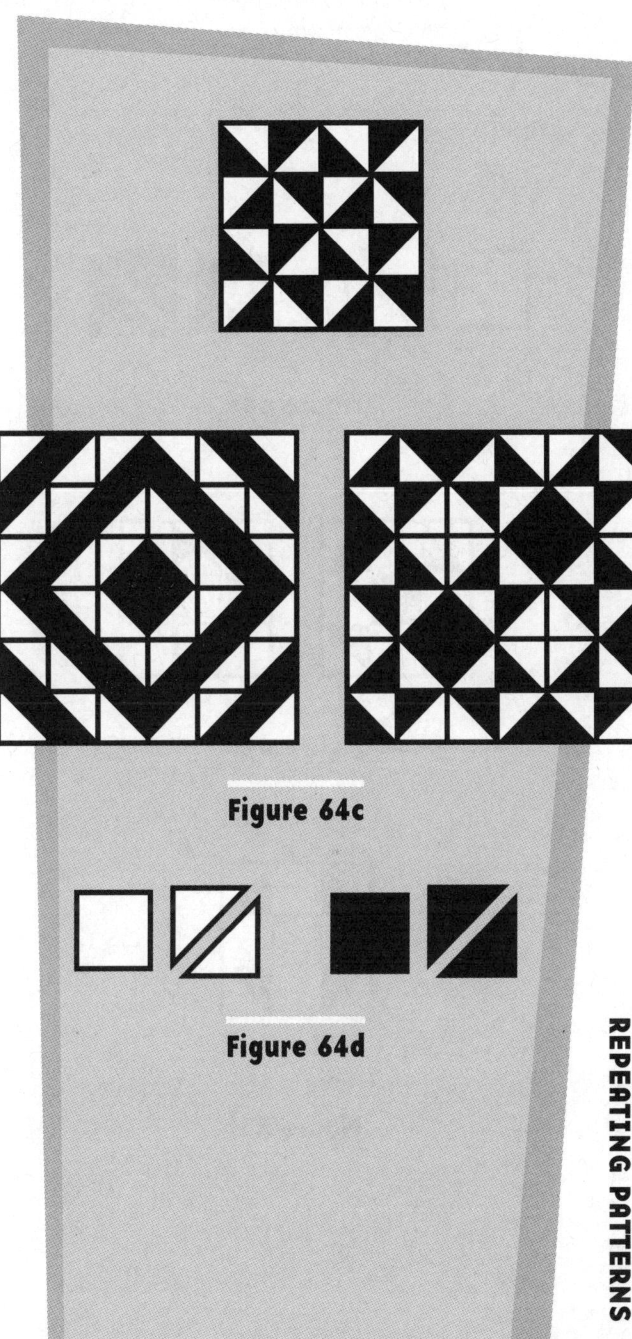

Figure 64c

Figure 64d

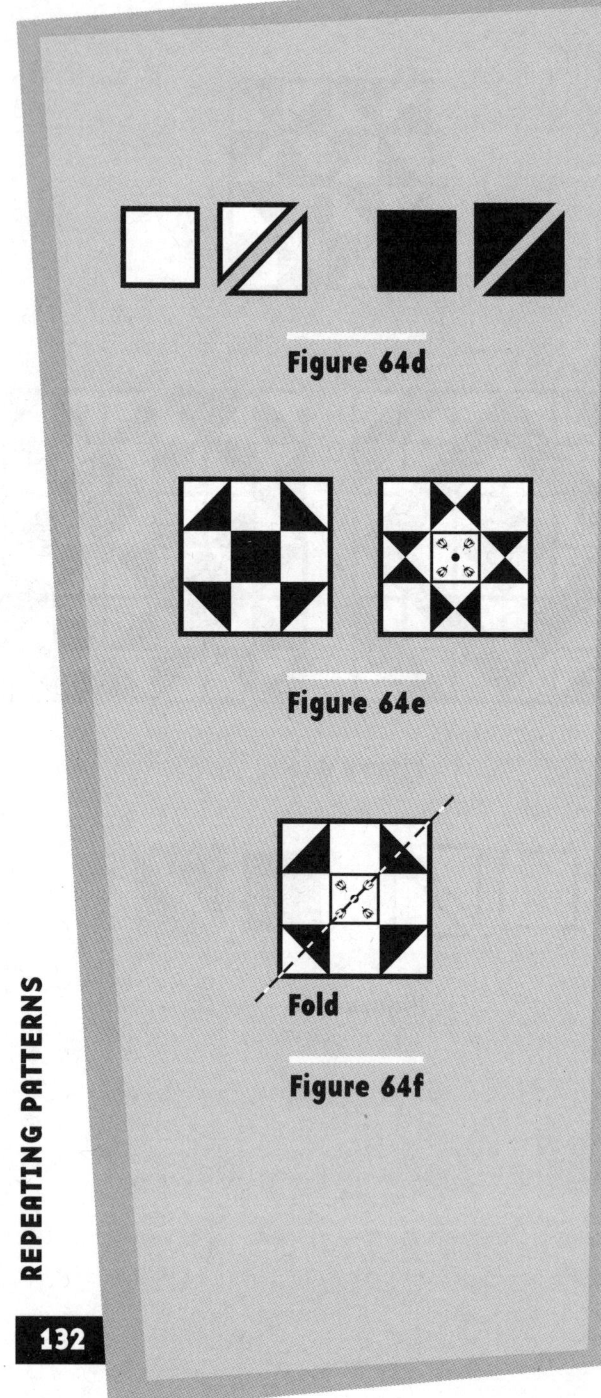

Figure 64d

Figure 64e

Figure 64f

THINGS TO DO

You can make interesting three-by-three quilt blocks. Each block will have nine squares. You need two sheets of paper in two different colors. Cut out nine squares of one color and nine squares of another color. Take four squares of each color and cut each square into two triangles. **Figure 64d**

Combine the squares and triangles to make a three-by-three quilt block. These are two traditional quilt blocks. They are called "Shoo Fly" and "Ohio Star." **Figure 64e**

Both have symmetry. Look at each quilt block. Find four different turn positions. Then find four different fold lines. (See page 116 for a discussion of these terms.) Here is one fold line, a diagonal. **Figure 64f**

Sew a patchwork quilt cover out of cloth. First plan it on paper. When you cut the fabric, allow an extra centimeter all around for the seams.

Read books about quilts. Some describe different kinds of quilts in various cultures and how to make them. *The Quilt-Block History of Pioneer Days, with Projects Kids Can Make,* written for children by Mary Cobb, gives instructions in quilting. There are also children's storybooks that describe the importance of quilts in the lives of the characters. One example is Deborah Hopkinson's *Sweet Clara and the Freedom Quilt.*

AdinKra Cloth from Ghana

This cloth is full of designs. Each design is a symbol—it stands for an idea. The Asante (also called Ashanti) people of Ghana, in West Africa, call the cloth *adinkra,* a word that means "saying good-bye." Long ago this was a special cloth for funerals, but it is now worn at any time. **Figure 65a**

An Asante cloth maker makes stamps by cutting the designs into pieces of calabash, the hard shell of a fruit. He attaches handles to these stamps and dips them in black dye. The cloth is divided into rectangles. Each rectangle of cloth has a different symbol stamped on it in neat rows.

Here are some of the symbols and their meaning. **Figure 65b**

MATERIALS

- **Sponges or potatoes sliced in half**
- **Knife**
- **Washable paint or dye (black or another dark color)**
- **Shallow, flat pan**
- **Several sheets of paper**
- **Old newspapers**
- **Length of white cloth**

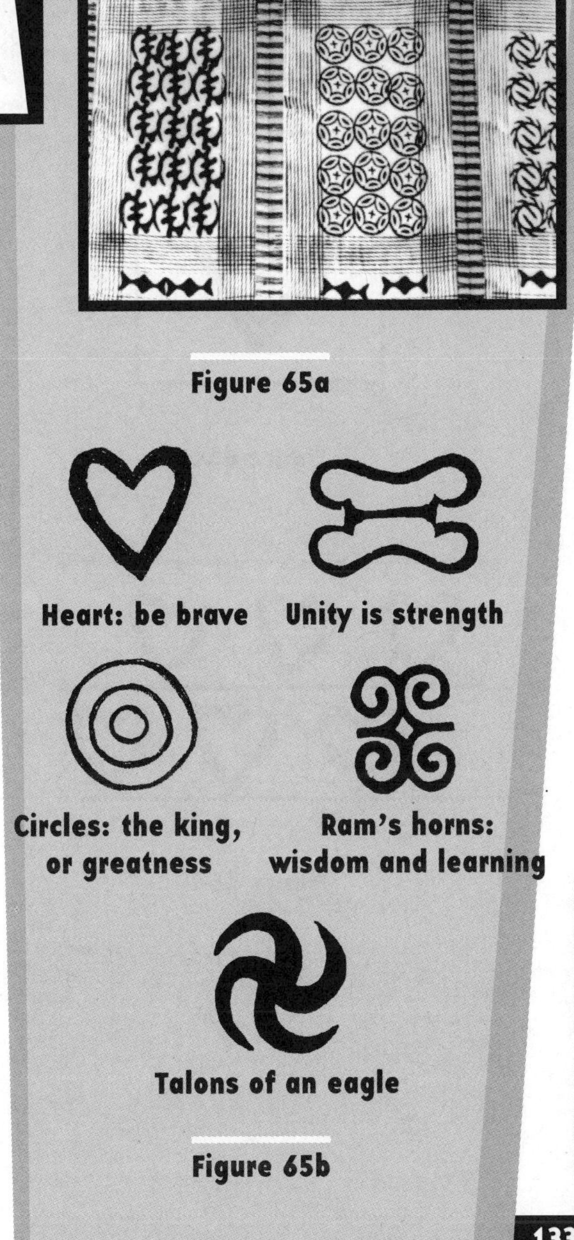

Figure 65a

Figure 65b

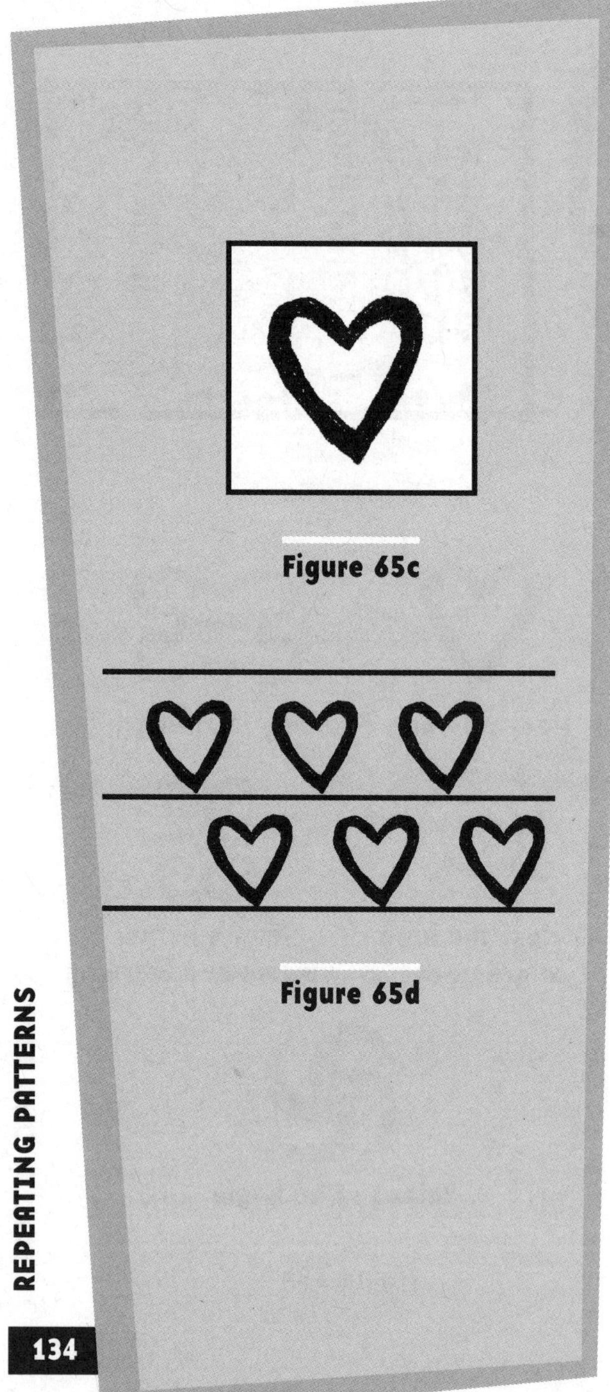
Figure 65c

Figure 65d

MAKING AN ADINKRA CLOTH

1. Start with an easy symbol, like the heart. Ask a grown-up to help you cut the design on the sponge or the cut half of the potato. **Figure 65c**
2. Pour paint or dye into the pan.
3. Place newspapers under a sheet of paper. Stamp the designs in several neat rows on the sheet of paper. If it's hard to place the symbols in a straight row, draw lines lightly in pencil on the paper before you start. **Figure 65d**
4. Choose another symbol and follow directions 1 through 3.
5. After you have practiced with symbols on paper, try to work on cloth.

THINGS TO THINK ABOUT AND DO

As you stamp the design, you must be careful that all the symbols go the same way. Tops and bottoms must be lined up. Look at each symbol. Can you turn the stamp and still have the symbol come out correct? In how many different positions can you turn each stamp so that it still looks the same? In other words, in how many positions is there turn symmetry for each of these symbols?

Look at the symbols: Heart, Unity, Talons, Ram's horns, and Circles.

Suppose you cut each symbol into a stencil and traced the design. Which symbols would not come out correct if you flipped the stencil over before you traced the design? Check your conclusions with the answers in Chapter 10.

Make a real Adinkra cloth using several different symbols. Design a set of symbols that stand for ideas that are important to you. Decorate greeting cards and other things with these symbols.

Tessellations in Islamic Culture

This beautiful pattern is made of colored tiles inlaid on a flat surface. This form of inlaid art is called *mosaic.* The tiles cover the entire surface, with no overlapping. Imagine how well the artist had to plan to make everything fit. Notice that the same design is repeated several times. The repetition of shapes to cover a surface is called a tessellation. This picture shows only a small section of a large wall. Islamic artists covered the walls of mosques and palaces with such mosaics. **Figure 66**

The religion of Islam developed in the Middle East in the seventh century. It spread eastward to India and other countries in Asia, and north and west to parts of Africa and to Spain and Turkey.

Islamic artists used mainly three types of decorations—geometric shapes, flowers, and calligraphy (writing in Arabic script). Some branches of the Islamic religion did not allow pictures of human beings or animals. Artists drew the geometric patterns using only a compass and a straightedge (an unmarked ruler). Many mosaics were made entirely of polygons, such as triangles, squares, parallelograms, and hexagons (six-sided shapes).

Figure 66

THINGS TO THINK ABOUT

Name the different polygons that you see in the pattern of inlaid work. How many different sizes and shapes of triangles can you find? How many different sizes of squares do you see? Can squares have different shapes? Can you find stars of different sizes? How many points are on each star? What other shapes do you see?

A collection of pattern blocks is ideal for making tessellations. You can buy a set in a school supply store or from a catalog, or you can make your own.

Polygon Patterns Islamic

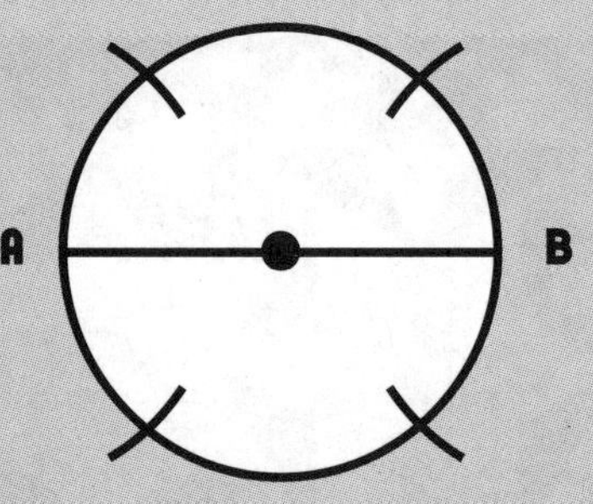

Figure 67a

Figure 67b

Follow in the footsteps of Islamic artists as you create wonderful patterns with polygons.

MATERIALS

- **Sheet of plain paper**
- **Compass**
- **Pencil**
- **Ruler or straightedge**
- **Scissors**
- **Piece of cardboard or Styrofoam**
- **Glue**
- **4 sheets of construction paper in 4 different colors**

MAKING A SET OF BLOCKS

1. Mark a point on a sheet of plain paper. Open the compass to a radius of about 1½ inches (4cm). Place the point of the compass on the point you marked and draw a circle. Draw a diameter from point A to point B. **Figure 67a**
2. Place the compass on point A and draw two arcs that intersect the circle. Do the same at point B. Connect the six points on the circle to form a hexagon. Cut it out. Glue it to the cardboard or Styrofoam and cut around it. Now you have a pattern to draw regular hexagons—all the sides have equal length and each angle measures 120 degrees. **Figure 67b**
3. Draw several hexagons on each sheet of construction paper. We'll call the colors of the paper yellow, red, green, and blue, but any colors are OK. Cut out the set of yellow hexagons.

4. Draw a diameter on each red hexagon. Cut out each hexagon and cut it in half. You now have a set of red trapezoids.
5. Draw all three diameters on each green hexagon. Cut out each hexagon and cut it in sixths. You now have a set of green equilateral triangles. All the sides are of equal length and the angles have equal measure—sixty degrees.
6. Draw three diameters on each blue hexagon. Cut out each hexagon and cut it in thirds. You now have a set of blue rhombuses (rhombi). **Figure 67c**

THINGS TO THINK ABOUT AND DO

Work with each shape separately. Can you cover a surface with only triangles? With only rhombi? With only trapezoids? With only hexagons? We call this *tessellating the plane.*

Try to tessellate the plane with two shapes—for example, triangles and hexagons. Can you form six-pointed stars? Islamic artists started in one place and then spread out from that point in all directions. What other combinations of shapes will tessellate the plane? **Figure 67d**

Glue your best tessellation to a sheet of construction paper. If you use commercial pattern blocks, trace the shapes on a sheet of plain paper and color them to make a beautiful mosaic.

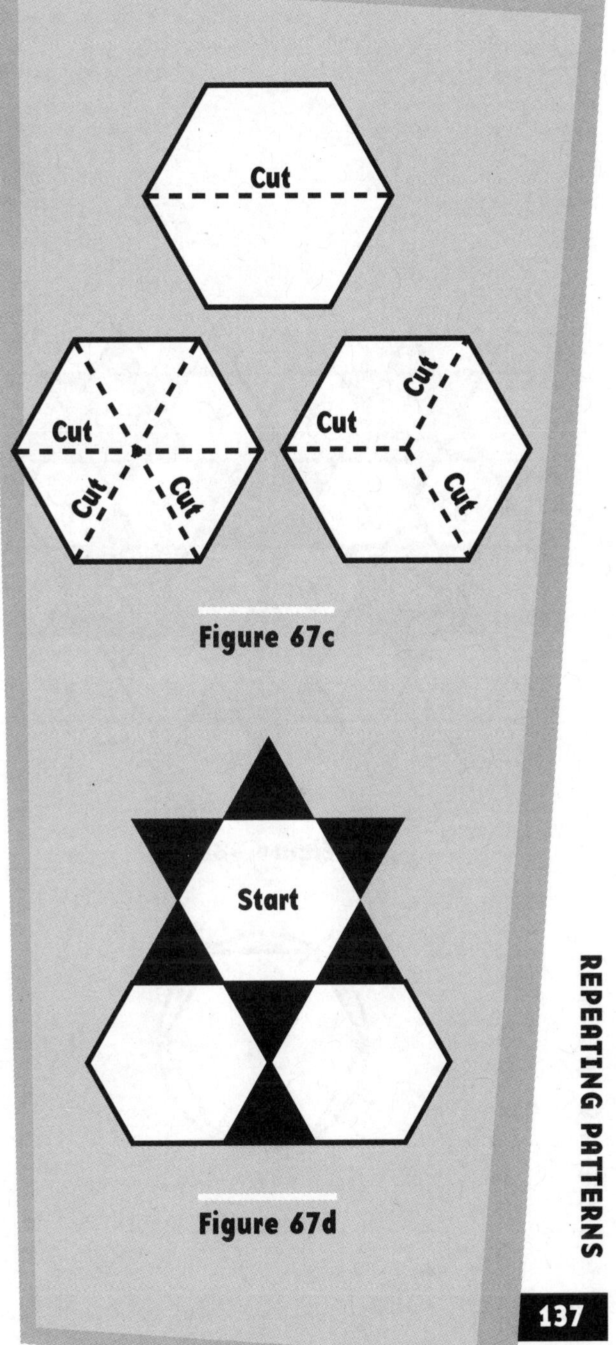

Figure 67c

Figure 67d

Be A Tessellation Artist Islamic

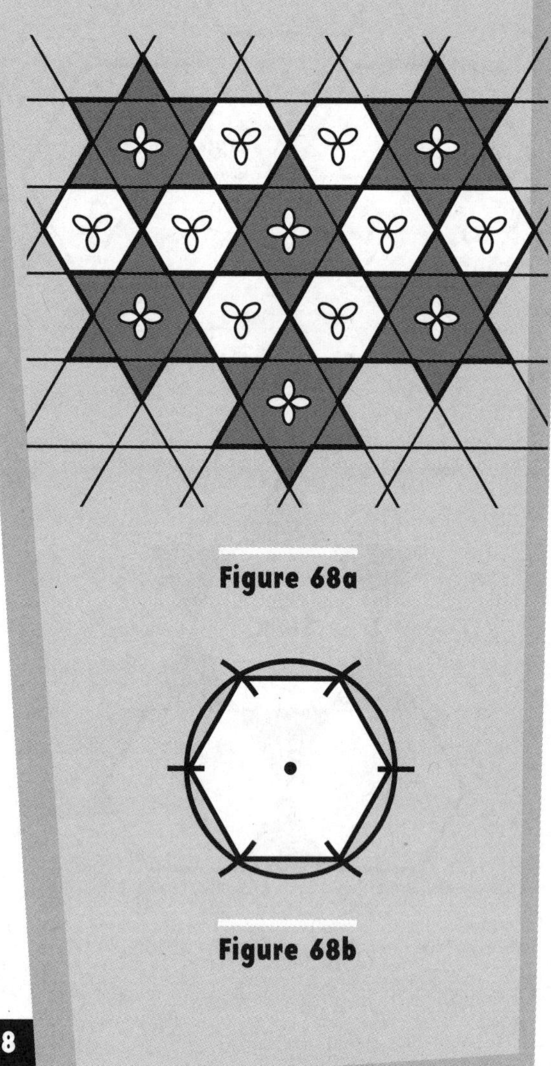

Figure 68a

Figure 68b

You can learn to draw tessellations using only a compass and a straightedge, like the Islamic artists. This tessellation is made of equilateral triangles and regular hexagons. **Figure 68a**

MATERIALS

- **Large sheets of paper**
- **Compass**
- **Pencil**
- **Ruler or straightedge**
- **Colored markers or crayons**

DRAWING A TESSELLATION

You will start by constructing a regular hexagon using a compass and a straightedge. Then you will draw the six equilateral triangles to form a six-pointed star. With this star as the center, you can repeat the design in all directions.

1. Follow the directions on page 136 to construct a hexagon. Draw the construction lines lightly in pencil. **Figure 68b**
2. Extend the lines that form the sides of the hexagon. Now you have a six-pointed star. **Figure 68c**
3. Erase the circle, the hexagon, and the construction marks. Outline the star with a heavy pencil line. **Figure 68d**

4. Draw six hexagons around the star. Here are directions to draw one hexagon. Use the same opening (radius) of the compass as in Step number 1.
   a. Place the point of the compass on the tip of the star at point A, and draw an arc at point C.
   b. Place the point of the compass on the tip of the star at point B, and draw an arc at point D.
   c. Then draw arcs from points C and D that intersect at point E. Draw a line through points C and E. Draw another line through points D and E. **Figure 68e**
   d. You now have a hexagon. Draw a heavy pencil line to outline it.
   e. Follow the directions above to draw five more hexagons around the star. You will find that you have already drawn some of the lines you need. You have also constructed many more triangles.

5. Continue as far as you can. Color the stars in one color and the hexagons in another color. Islamic artists liked to draw flowers in the center of each shape.

Don't be discouraged if your pattern is a bit lopsided. This craft takes a lot of patience. Keep at it, and you will have a beautiful work of art!

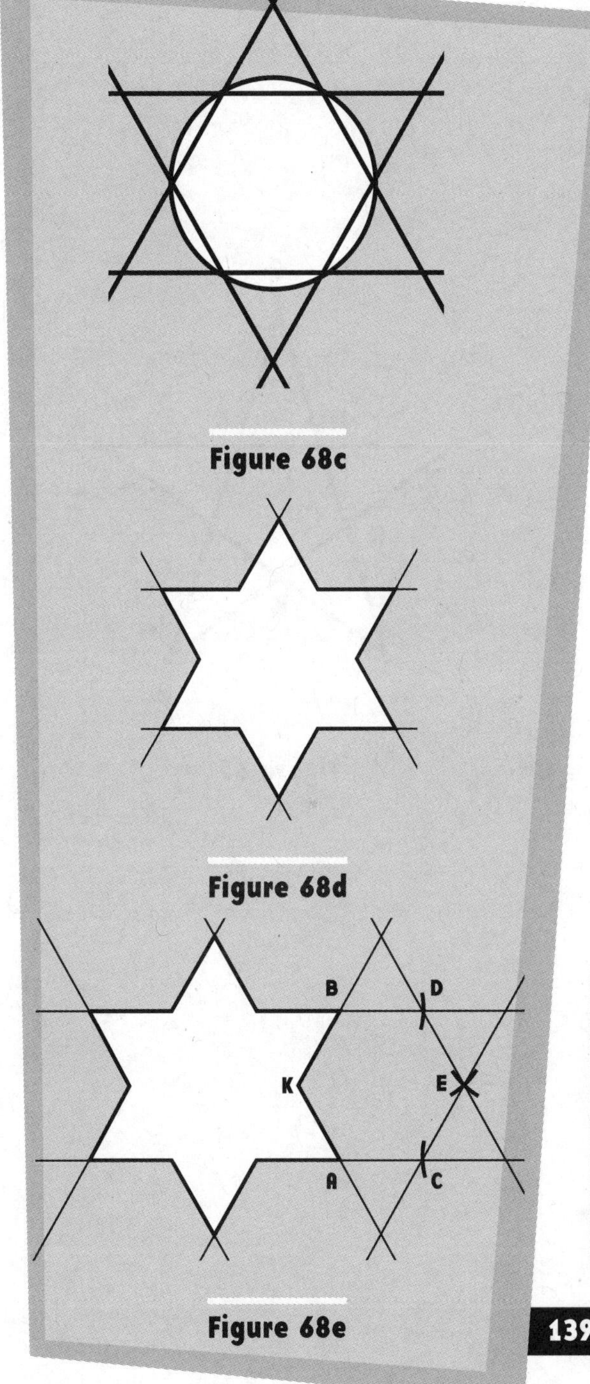

Figure 68c

Figure 68d

Figure 68e

10

Selected Answers

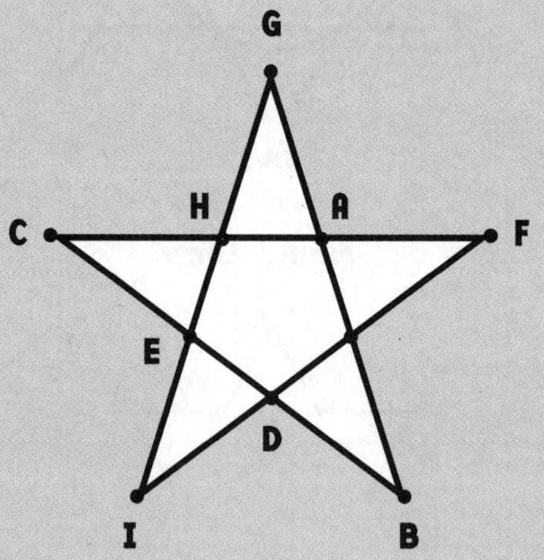

Figure 69

You will not find many answers in this section of the book. That's because most of the activities are self-checking and you are smart enough to figure out the reasons if something doesn't work out. For example, if the rows and columns of a magic square don't add up correctly, you can try to find your mistake rather than looking for an answer in the back of the book. That's a lot more fun, and it gives you a feeling of success.

CHAPTER 3

Page 36, Pentalpha. This is really a puzzle rather than a game. One solution is to place the counters on the points of the game board in alphabetical order, as shown in this diagram. Begin with point A and end with point I. **Figure 69**

CHAPTER 5

Page 72, Rice Multiplies. On the eleventh day, the wise man receives 1,024 grains. Multiply 2 X 2 X 2 X . . . X 2 [10 factors] $=2^{10}$.

On the twenty-first day, the wise man should receive 2^{20} grains of rice. This number is the same as 2^{10} X 2^{10} or 1,024 X 1,024. To get a quick estimate, round the number 1,024 to 1,000. Then multiply 1,000 X 1,000 = 1,000,000, or one million. The exact answer is 1,048,576 grains of rice.

On the thirty-first day, the wise man should receive 2^{30} grains of rice. This number is the same as 2^{10} X 2^{10} X 2^{10}. The exact answer is 1,073,741,824 grains. An easy number that is close to the exact answer is 1,000,000 X 1,000 = 1,000,000,000, or one billion grains of rice. The wise man didn't ask for much, did he?

CHAPTER 6

Page 79, Crossing the River in the Sea Islands. Jonah must make three trips. He might have taken the duck first, then gone back for the fox and the corn.

Page 81, Crossing the River in Liberia. This is one way to get all the objects across in seven trips. Another way is to interchange the leopard and the cassava leaves. **Figure 70**

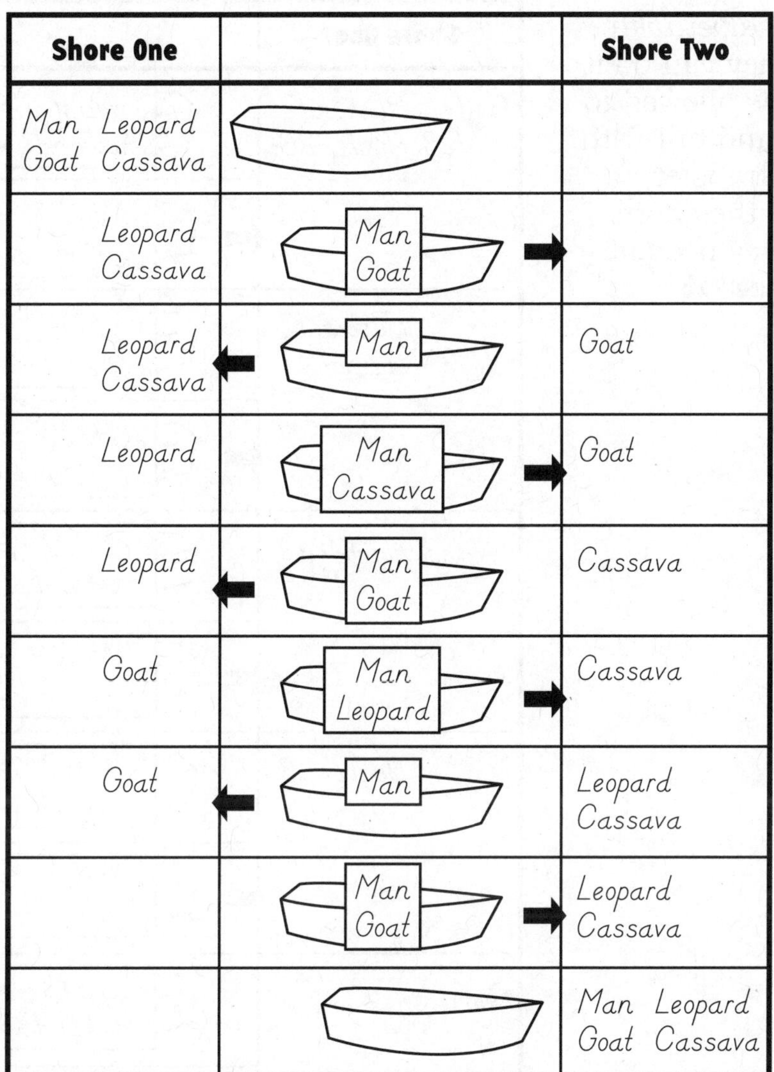

Shore One		Shore Two
Man Leopard Goat Cassava		
Leopard Cassava	Man Goat →	
Leopard Cassava	← Man	Goat
Leopard	Man Cassava →	Goat
Leopard	← Man Goat	Cassava
Goat	Man Leopard →	Cassava
Goat	← Man	Leopard Cassava
	Man Goat →	Leopard Cassava
		Man Leopard Goat Cassava

Figure 70

Page 82, Crossing the River with Jealous Husbands. They can do it in nine trips if a wife is allowed to be without her hus-band but with another man as they transfer between the boat and the shore. **Figure 71a** Otherwise they need at least eleven trips. **Figure 71b**

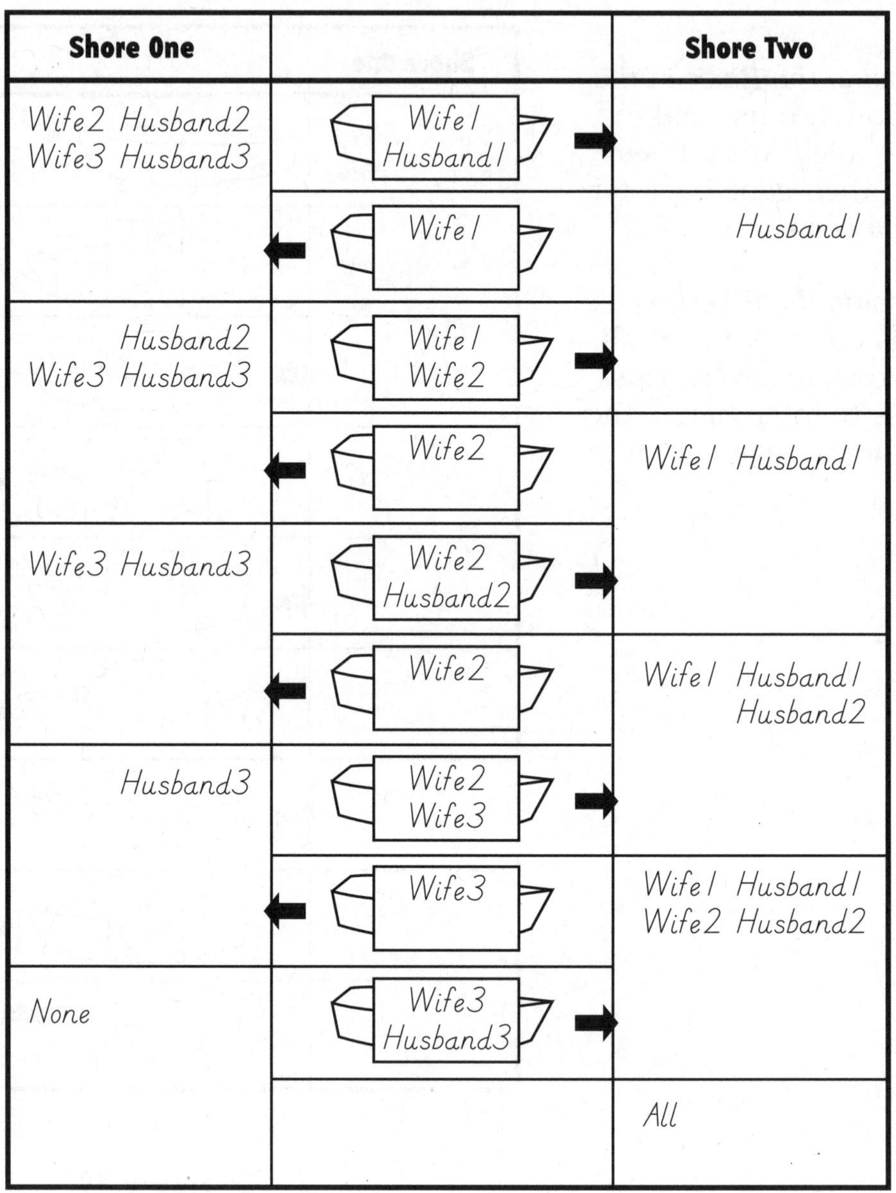

Shore One		Shore Two
Wife2 Husband2 Wife3 Husband3	Wife1 Husband1 →	
	← Wife1	Husband1
Husband2 Wife3 Husband3	Wife1 Wife2 →	
	← Wife2	Wife1 Husband1
Wife3 Husband3	Wife2 Husband2 →	
	← Wife2	Wife1 Husband1 Husband2
Husband3	Wife2 Wife3 →	
	← Wife3	Wife1 Husband1 Wife2 Husband2
None	Wife3 Husband3 →	
		All

Figure 71a

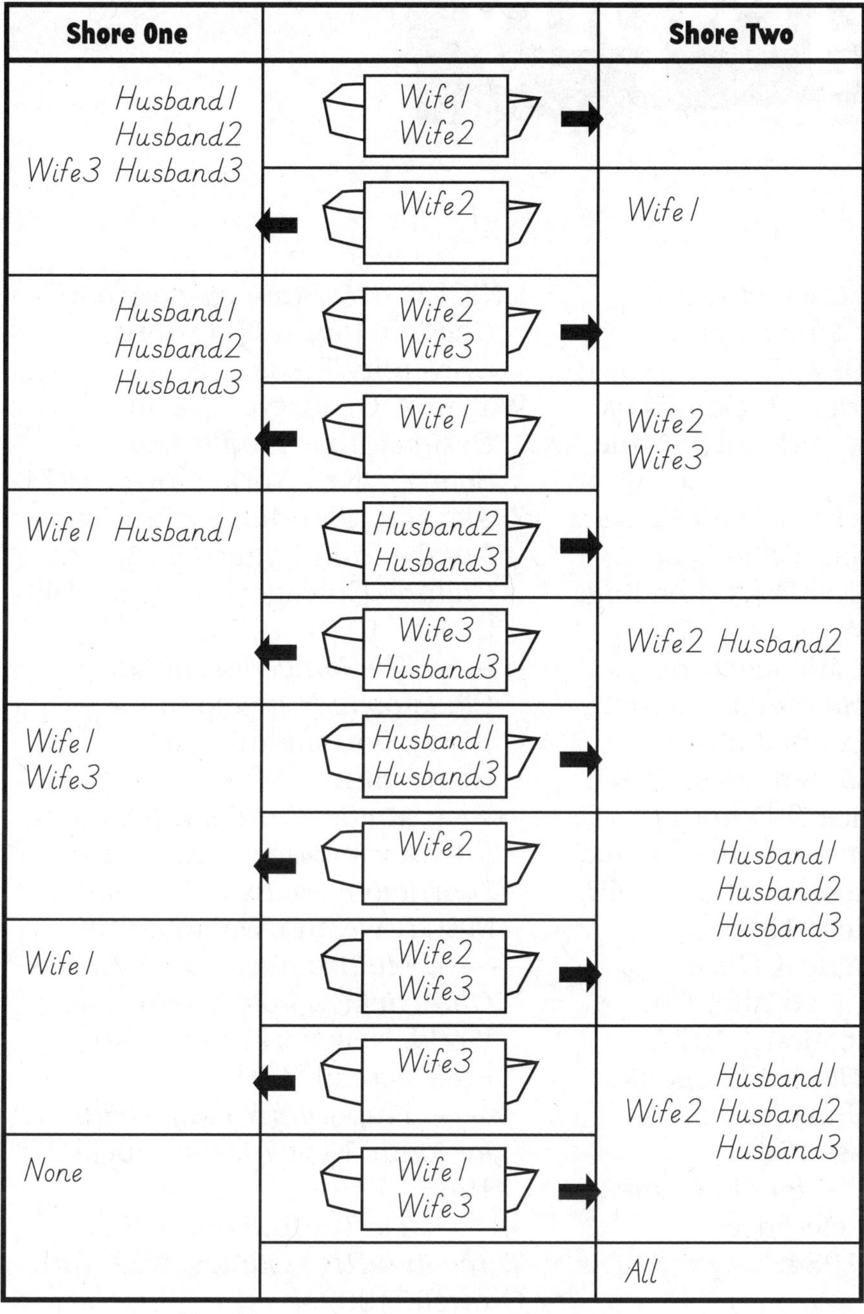

Figure 71b

CHAPTER 9

Page 125, The Washington Covenant Belt. There are approximately 13,000 beads.

Page 127, African Patterns from Congo. The smallest stamp has half of the design, while the smallest stencil has one-quarter of the design. You can flip over the stencil, but not the stamp. Of course, it may be more convenient to put the complete design on the stamp or stencil.

Page 133, Adinkra Cloth. Turn symmetry (including the starting position): Heart, one; Unity, two; Talons, four; Ram's horns, two; Circles, infinite.

If you flipped the stencils, the talons would curve in the opposite direction, but the other symbols would come out right.

Bibliography

BOOKS FOR ADULTS

Appleton, Leroy. *American Indian Design and Decoration.* New York: Dover, 1971.

Ascher, Marcia. *Ethnomathematics: A Multi-cultural View of Mathematical Ideas.* Belmont, CA: Brooks/ Cole, 1991.

Bell, Robbie & Michael Cornelius. *Board Games Round the World.* New York: Cambridge University Press, 1988.

Bourgoin, J. *Arabic Geometrical Pattern and Design.* New York: Dover, 1973.

Centner, Th. *L'enfant Africain et ses Jeux.* Elisabethville, Congo: CEPSI, 1963.

Crane, Louise. *African Games of Strategy.* Urbana: University of Illinois, 1982.

Culin, Stewart. *Games of the North American Indians,* 1907. Reprint: Dover, 1975.

Dolber, Sam M. *From Computation to Recreation.* Atwater, CA: Author, 1980.

Gerdes, Paulus. *Geometrical Recreations of Africa.* Paris: Harmattan, 1997.

Grunfeld, Frederic, ed. *Games of the World.* New York: Ballantine, 1975.

Kenschaft, Patricia C. *Math Power: How to Help Your Child Love Math, Even If You Don't.* Reading, MA: Addison-Wesley, 1997.

Krause, Marina. *Multicultural Mathematics Materials.* Reston, VA: National Council of Teachers of Mathematics, 1983.

Lumpkin, Beatrice & Dorothy Strong. *Multicultural Science and Math Connections.* Portland, ME: J. Weston Walch, 1995.

McConville, Robert. *A History of Board Games.* Palo Alto, CA: Creative Publications, 1974.

Neihardt, J. G. *Black Elk Speaks.* Lincoln, NE: University of Nebraska Press, 1961.

Russ, Laurence. *Mankala Games.* Algonac, MI: Reference Publications, 1984.

UNICEF. *The State of the World's Children* (annual). Oxford University Press.

Williams, Geoffrey. *African Designs from Traditional Sources.* New York: Dover, 1971.

Zaslavsky, Claudia. *Africa Counts: Number and Pattern in African Culture.* Chicago: Lawrence Hill Books, 1973, 1979.

———. *The Multicultural Math Classroom: Bringing in the World.* Portsmouth, NH: Heinemann, 1996.

———. *Multicultural Mathematics: Interdisciplinary Cooperative-Learning Activities.* Portland, ME: J. Weston Walch, 1993.

———. *Multicultural Math: Hands-On Activities from around the World.* New York: Scholastic Professional, 1994.

———. *Preparing Young Children for Math.* New York: Schocken, 1986.

———. *Tic Tac Toe and Other Three-in-a-Row Games.* New York: Crowell, 1982.

BOOKS FOR KIDS

Birch, David. *The King's Chessboard.* New York: Dial, 1988. Growth by doubling, in an old tale from India, Persia, and China.

Carlson, Laurie. *More than Moccasins: A Kid's Activity Guide to Traditional North American Indian Life.* Chicago Review Press, 1994.

Cobb, Mary. *The Quilt-Block History of Pioneer Days, with Projects Kids Can Make.* Brookfield, CT: The Millbrook Press, 1995.

Coerr, Eleanor. *Sadako and the Thousand Paper Cranes.* New York: Putnam, 1993.

Corwin, J. H. *African Crafts.* New York: Franklin Watts, 1990.

D'Amato, Janet & Alex. *Indian Crafts.* Toronto: McLeod, 1968.

Ernst, Lisa Campbell. *Sam Johnson and the Blue Ribbon Quilt.* New York: William Morrow, 1983.

———. *The Tangram Magician.* New York: Harry Abrams, 1990.

Flournoy, Valerie. *The Patchwork Quilt.* New York: Dutton, 1985.

Graymont, Barbara. *The Iroquois.* New York: Chelsea, 1988.

Grifalconi, Ann. *The Village of Round and Square Houses.* Boston: Little, Brown, 1987.

Hopkinson, Deborah. *Sweet Clara and the Freedom Quilt.* New York: Knopf, 1993.

Kohl, Herbert. *Insides, Outsides, Loops, and Lines.* New York: Freeman, 1995.

Millard, Anne. *Pyramids: Egyptian, Nubian, Mayan, Aztec, Modern.* New York: Kingfisher, 1996.

Neale, Robert. *Origami Plain and Simple.* New York: St. Martin's Griffen, 1994.

Orlando, Louise. *The Multicultural Game Book.* New York: Scholastic Professional, 1993.

Osofsky, Audrey. *Dream Catcher.* New York: Orchard Books, 1992.

Pittman, Helena C. *A Grain of Rice.* New York: Hastings House, 1986. Based on a Chinese folk tale about growth by doubling.

Temko, Florence. *Traditional Crafts from Africa.* Minneapolis: Lerner, 1996.

Tompert, Ann. *Grandfather Tang's Story.* New York: Crown, 1990. About tangrams.

Yue, Charlotte & David. *The Pueblo.* Houghton Mifflin, 1986.

———. *The Tipi.* Boston: Houghton Mifflin, 1984.

Zaslavsky, Claudia. *Tic Tac Toe and Other Three-in-a-Row Games.* New York: Crowell, 1982.

A WORD ABOUT UNICEF

UNICEF, the United Nations Children's Fund, is an organization that helps children around the world. They help fight hunger and disease among poor and sick children, work to end child labor, expand opportunities for education, and deal with many other issues.

Children in this country can do many things. For example, with a treatment called Oral Rehydration Therapy, or ORT for short, you can prevent a child's death from severe diarrhea. ORT is a mixture of salt, sugar, and clean water. Can you guess the cost of one ORT treatment? It is just eight cents, much less than the price of a candy bar. Some of the money you raise for UNICEF on Halloween goes for this treatment. ORT saves the lives of one million children every year, but millions more die for lack of the treatment.

UNICEF is also concerned with child labor. More than 250 million children between the ages of five and fourteen are made to work long hours under terrible conditions, and do not have a chance to go to school. They make soccer balls, sew clothing, and work on farms. This happens even in rich countries like the United States.

You can get involved and help children less fortunate than yourself by asking a parent or teacher to contact the UNICEF office in your area or contact the U.S. Committee for UNICEF, 333 East 38th Street, New York, NY 10016; telephone (212) 686-5522; fax (212) 779-1679. UNICEF will send kits for fund-raising and other activities. Halloween is a great time to collect funds for UNICEF while you're out trick-or-treating with a parent or guardian. Always remember, children can make a difference.